# Be still and know

## Thinking with God

DayOne

© Day One Publications 2006
First printed 2006

ISBN 1-84625-001-3

9 781846 250019 >

Readings from an earlier work by Sheila Giffard Smith; in this edition, some changes
have been made by the publisher, with the approval of the author.

British Library Cataloguing in Publication Data available
Published by Day One Publications
Ryelands Road, Leominster, HR6 8NZ
☎ 01568 613 740 FAX 01568 611 473
email—sales@dayone.co.uk
web site—www.dayone.co.uk
North American—e-mail—sales@dayonebookstore.com
North American—web site—www.dayonebookstore.com

Designed by Steve Devane and printed by Gutenberg Press, Malta

## ACKNOWLEDGEMENTS

This book is dedicated to all those who have helped me on my spiritual journey.

I thank God for speaking so movingly to me through his Word over so many years.

## BE STILL

*Be still and know that I am God. I will be exalted in the earth.*
PSALM 46:10

God will be exalted among nations and on earth. Nothing can thwart his ultimate purposes. Therefore we can really be still and have inward peace, knowing that he is God, the omnipotent Creator and Redeemer, no matter how great the chaos reigning on earth might be.

God's Word assures us that this is true for each of us today. We may experience conflict, discord, suffering; but none of this can prevail against his purposes for the good of those who own his lordship.

## AUTHOR'S NOTE

This book is not designed to be read through at one sitting. Each short passage is the outcome of one morning's prayerful Bible Study. My hope is that you, the reader, will want to read for yourself the complete Bible passage from which each extract is taken, and allow God to speak to you personally. He may, and probably will, say something quite different to you, for he knows us individually with all our particular circumstances and needs. All he desires is an open mind and an open heart.

## LEARNER DRIVERS

*For this God is our God for ever and ever; he will be our guide even to the end.*

PSALM 48:14

To be a Christian can perhaps be compared with being a learner driver. The car is my earthly body, the vehicle containing my *self*. But now there are two people in it—the Lord Jesus and I.

This will be a journey with our Lord. I am at the wheel, because I have to learn to use the vehicle; but the Lord is certainly the Instructor. He knows the road, chooses the way, tells me when to apply the brake or press the accelerator, and he monitors my speed. The great thing is that he knows the vehicle!

In practical terms, everything may be in my hands, but always he is in ultimate control. Sometimes I am in danger, to myself or to others, having failed to slow down, or perhaps having taken my eyes off the road. Then—as in a dual-control car—he applies the brake for me, or takes control of the steering wheel.

If I take a wrong turning, thinking that I know the way better than he does, I cannot hold him responsible for the consequences. But, mercifully, he still goes with me. He will, at any time, direct me back on the right road if I ask him to. My part is to keep steadily on his course, and to be alert to the signs along the way and obey them. If I get into trouble, I involve him as well—there is a sense in which he suffers with me.

Along the way, we shall perhaps encounter difficulties. There will always be other people to consider, and I shall need to learn traffic sense. My Highway Code is the Bible, and I need a thorough knowledge of that.

Suppose I have engine trouble? Well, my Instructor is able to direct me to a reliable garage or an able mechanic. Sometimes he will even put the matter right himself, for nothing is too hard for him. There will never be an emergency which he cannot enable me to meet, no need that he cannot supply, no route too difficult for him to steer me through. Most important of all, since I am travelling with him I shall most certainly reach my destination. In this life we shall always be 'learner drivers', and the vehicle will probably be battered, scarred and worn out. But so what—we shall be THERE!

## LAMPS

*In the same way, let your light shine before men, that they may see your good deeds and praise your Father in heaven.*
MATTHEW 5:16

The obvious purpose of lamps is to shed light around. A great deal of darkness is dispelled by one light. This is an encouraging thought in view of the fact that Christians, who are to be light in the world, are in the minority.

It is sometimes depressing to realise how small the Church is, and how vast the powers of evil. We seem to think we must have more and more Christians if the Church is to be effective—that they must outnumber unbelievers to gain victory. But is this so? A lone Christian in an office, school or community may feel hopelessly outnumbered; but does a light bulb need to be as big as the room it lights? Of course not!

Just as a single light bulb no bigger than three inches in diameter can light up a room thousands of times larger than itself, so a Christian can uphold the truth and shed light upon the darkness, ignorance and sin all around him or her. So, too, the Church, small as it is, can shed the light of God to the farthest corners of the earth. Jesus himself is the Light of the World (John 8:12). His light is powerful indeed and will never go out. Lord grant that it will shine through you and me.

## HUMILITY

*Do nothing out of selfish ambition or vain conceit, but in humility consider others better than yourselves.*
PHILIPPIANS 2:3

Humility is not expecting praise, appreciation or gratitude. It is accepting hurt, misunderstanding, rejection and disappointment without surprise or resentment. It is to give and to love without thought of return. It is to see the dark side of life as God's opportunity for me to grow in grace and holiness, and to be thankful for it. It is to care supremely that God may delight in each step I take, and that he may be glorified in all. It is to love, above all else, to be with him in deep inner peace and joy.

## GOD'S WILL, NOT MINE

*The LORD forbid that I should lay a hand on the LORD's anointed.*
1 SAMUEL 26:11

In verses 1–12, we read of David's search for King Saul, who has become David's enemy. When he finds Saul asleep, David has an opportunity to kill him. Abishai had said, 'God has given your enemy into your hand.' David must surely have been tempted. But

God's will for us is never in conflict with his revealed word. He had certainly provided the opportunity and had caused Saul's men to sleep deeply (verse 12), but it was clearly not in his purpose that David should take advantage of the situation. Was he testing David? We do not know; but there is something we can learn here: God sometimes opens up a particular way only so that we may be strengthened by rejection of that way, bringing glory to his name.

We can never regard an open door as God's opportunity unless it tallies with our knowledge of God's will—and God's will is made known supremely in his Word.

## HOLY LANGUAGE

*We hear them declaring the wonders of God in our own tongues.*
ACTS 2:11

By the word 'them' is meant the eleven apostles, and possibly other believers, at the time of Pentecost. What were they saying in this gift of strange languages? Nothing to bring glory to themselves; they were glorifying God for his wonderful works. Whom do we worship and thank for the gifts we have? For whose benefit are they given? God does give us his gifts to enjoy; but how easy it is to become proud and boastful in these, and how tempting to use them selfishly! All are gifts from God himself, and the joy will be his if we use them in his service and the service of others, and for his glory.

We are stewards, only, of all we possess.

## THE GOOD OLD DAYS

*All the Israelites grumbled against Moses and Aaron: 'If only...'*
*'Why ...'*

NUMBERS 14:2–3

Like the Israelites, we tend to think in times of difficulty that we are worse off than ever before and we long for the 'good old days'. The Israelites continually forgot how great their hardship had been in Egypt, and every time they came up against difficulty they grumbled, forgetting the mercy of God. Could they not trust him to deliver them as before?

How easy it is in the Christian life to wish for the irresponsible slavery to self that we had before we knew Christ! Yes, things can be hard for the Christian; but nothing can ever again be so dark for us now that we are his. Our deliverance has begun. We have been set free.

Satan can, and will, pursue us and attack us from every quarter. What are we going to do then? Wail for our former bondage? No! Trust our Lord. He knows what he is doing—AND, he has promised to keep us to the end.


## BACKWARDS OR FORWARDS?

*Yet I hold this against you: You have forsaken your first love.*

REVELATION 2:4

*I know your deeds, your love and faith, your service and*
*perseverance, and that you are now doing more than you did at first.*

REVELATION 2:19

Of the church in Ephesus, it was said that they had forsaken the love they had at first. They were falling away, tragically going backwards. But of the church in Thyatira it was said that they were doing more now than at first.

Of how many Christians is it true that their love, faith, service and perseverance are on the increase? It is good to stop and take a good look at ourselves from time to time. Am I becoming slack in my Christian life? Then I need to pray earnestly for renewal. Am I growing steadily in spiritual stature—more like Jesus? Then I shall want to praise God with a thankful heart.

## SPIRITUAL FITNESS

*Physical training is of some value, but godliness has value for all things.*

1 TIMOTHY 4:8

Physical exercise is good only for our short lifespan. Spiritual exercise, on the other hand, leads to godliness, keeping us spiritually fit. It is profitable not only for this life, but also for all time, and in all things.

How do we keep spiritually fit? Regular Bible reading and prayer are essential exercises, and we can add to these the service of others, and adopting a simple, disciplined lifestyle. Godliness does not come cheap—and we shall need to persevere.

## GOD'S UNEXPECTED REMEDY

*Just as Moses lifted up the snake in the desert, so the Son of Man must be lifted up, that everyone who believes in him may have eternal life.*

JOHN 3:14–15

Jesus is referring to the time when the Lord sent venomous snakes among the grumbling Israelites. When they begged Moses to pray that the snakes would go away, the Lord told Moses to set up a pole with a bronze snake on it. Then, when anyone bitten by a snake looked up at the bronze replica, he lived.

We note that God did not take away the snakes, as the people asked. Instead, he gave them a remedy which they themselves could use. In a similar way, when Jesus died for us, God did not remove sin from the world; he gave us a remedy to be appropriated by each person individually.

To look to Christ is to have him take away my sin. It is vital that I believe in him. No one else can give me what I need to save me.

## GOD'S TIME AND OURS

*But do not forget this one thing, dear friends: With the Lord a day is like a thousand years, and a thousand years are like a day.*

2 PETER 3:8

If, as we are told in the Bible, to God a thousand years are but a day, then it is only two days since Christ walked this earth and worked his miracles; two days since Pentecost; two days since God's promises were given to us through the lips of Jesus and his apostles! How can we think that Christianity is outdated, not applicable in our present day of speed and innovation? God is immortal, and his power does not diminish with time. It was but a few days ago to him that he divided the waters of the Red Sea so that his chosen people could cross over; only the day before yesterday that he himself came into the world in the person of Jesus Christ. God is alive and active today!

Our eyes may be blinded, encrusted with the sin of thousands of years; but HIS eyes are not dimmed, nor ever will they be. If we turn to him, he will restore our spiritual sight, and our perspective. We shall see his glory, just as Moses did. We can receive his power, just as the early believers did. And then we shall be able to give all, for Jesus' sake.

## SEEING IN THE DARK

*He [God] knows what lies in darkness.*
DANIEL 2:22

The Book of Daniel is full of spiritual treasure. Right at the beginning, we read that Jehoiakim, king of Judah, is taken captive by Nebuchadnezzar, king of Babylon, and that this was the Lord's doing. The people must have thought God had deserted them. A seemingly bad start! But an amazing train of events is set in motion.

There are good things we can take to ourselves in all that, especially, perhaps, the words from chapter two, where we read that God knows what lies in darkness. So often we cannot know what is happening in our lives; we cannot see in the darkness. It may be the darkness of bereavement, or fear, desertion, insecurity or illness. We cry out, 'How can I know the way?' But we do not always need to see in the darkness—'The Lord turns my darkness into light' (2 Samuel 22:29). Jesus says of himself that he is the light of the world, and he is the way. What we need is not better sight or 'spiritual spectacles', but trust—trust in God's knowledge of the darkness and what is within it, and trust in God himself.

Often, after a time of suffering, we can recognise that God

allowed it in order to bestow a greater blessing. Then is there any limit to what we are willing to bear, knowing that all is from the hand of a loving and all-wise Heavenly Father? He delights to give his children more than they can ever desire or deserve. So, in times of darkness and distress, we can say in trust, 'I thank and praise you, my God.'


## I, A SINNER?

*I know my transgressions, and my sin is always before me.*
PSALM 51:3

This whole psalm is full of lament for the writer's own sinfulness, and his intense desire for God's cleansing.

If we fail to recognise sin in ourselves, it may be that we are weighing up ourselves against others, judging by the world's standards. By comparison, we think, we are not too bad. 'Sin' is an ugly word, we say, and it surely doesn't apply to us—we haven't murdered anybody!

This sort of comparison is deceptive and worthless. The psalmist realises the truth when he says to God, 'Against you, you only, have I sinned and done what is evil in your sight.' 'In *your* sight'—it is how we are before a holy God that is important.

Only as we discover God through a sinless Christ do we begin to recognise the full extent of our sinfulness and need. Jesus Christ alone is our touchstone, our only standard. When we measure ourselves against him, we will sincerely echo the psalmist's words: 'I know my transgressions.'

## THE INVALID AT THE POOL OF BETHESDA—JOHN 5:1–18

*Here a great number of disabled people used to lie—the blind, the lame, the paralysed. One who was there had been an invalid for thirty-eight years. When Jesus saw him lying there and learned that he had been in this condition for a long time, he asked him, 'Do you want to get well?'*

JOHN 5:3–6

For years, this sick man had been lying by the pool, waiting for someone to lift him into the water when it was stirred up—a picture of passivity and dependence. When Jesus sees him, he asks a seemingly obvious question: 'Do you want to get well?'

Did Jesus suspect that the man enjoyed his inactivity? He did later tell the man to stop sinning, but we do not know what the sin was. Now, though, he gives the man three active commands: RISE, TAKE, WALK! Jesus demands of this man obedience without faith. We can perhaps imagine the invalid's thoughts: 'How can I rise, pick up my mat and walk? I haven't walked for thirty-eight years. Wait! I do feel strength coming into my legs, my whole body. Perhaps I could just manage to stand. I can! I can even walk! I'll get rid of this mat.' Strength came in response to obedience.

In the same way, Jesus may ask of us the seemingly impossible. He knows our feelings of weakness, helplessness and uselessness. But when he commands, we can be sure of our ability to obey, relying on his strength. He knows that is all we need.

## TROUBLED WATERS

*When evening came, the disciples ... got into a boat and set off across the lake for Capernaum.*

JOHN 6:16–21

We do not know why the disciples left Jesus and set out on their own, but as they were crossing the lake, a storm blew up. Doubtless, they were anxious and distressed. Jesus came to them 'walking on the water'. We are told that they were then 'willing to take him into the boat', and they quickly reached the shore. This little episode has a lesson for us: Of course we get into difficulty when we leave Jesus out of our lives. Our little craft is in danger, but Jesus knows. He graciously comes to us, walking on the troubled waters of our circumstances. If we willingly receive him into our problems, he will restore calm, and we shall be sure of making progress and reaching the shore.

## FREEDOM

*I am the gate; whoever enters through me will be saved. He will come in and go out.*

JOHN 10:9

Notice the freedom Christ offers his flock—freedom to come and go under the watchful eye of the Shepherd.

In stark contrast, those bound by Satan are *prisoners*, driven by him to destruction. The Lord Jesus does not drive people; he leads his flock, as the shepherds in the East lead their sheep. If we follow, it is because he sets our will free to do so.

While our Good Shepherd leads us, we need fear neither the journey, nor the destination.

## GOD'S SUFFICIENCY—DANIEL 9:1–27

*... we have sinned and done wrong. We have been wicked and have rebelled; we have turned away from your commands and laws.*

DANIEL 9:5

In this chapter, there is a marvellous picture of God's sufficiency in the face of our sinfulness and inadequacy.

Daniel is praising God: He keeps his covenant and steadfast love towards those who love and obey him; he is righteous, merciful and forgiving. God, then, is exactly the one his people need: They have sinned, so they need his mercy; they have broken their covenant with God—suffering calamity as a consequence—and now they need to confess their disobedience and call upon God for his forgiveness. The only one to whom they can turn is God. But God is righteous, and they are sinners, so how can they approach him? Only on the grounds of his mercy.

Are we not in a similar position? We are sinners, and we are unworthy to approach God. But all that God was to the people of Daniel's day, he is to us today. In the covenant of grace, because of the work of Christ at Calvary, we can put our trust in him to repair our damaged lives, for he desires this so that he may be glorified in us.

## FEARFUL SERVANTS

*God has said, 'Never will I leave you; never will I forsake you.' So*

*we say with confidence, 'The Lord is my helper; I will not be afraid. What can man do to me?'*
HEBREWS 13:5–6

Several of God's chosen servants in the Bible display a total lack of confidence when faced with a God-given task: Moses, Gideon, Jonah, Saul and others. Certainly they were not equal to, or worthy of, that work in their own strength; nor were the disciples of Jesus, and nor are we. But just as God said to the fearful men, 'Don't be afraid; I will be with you', so he promises us his presence and strength.

Before his death, Jesus told his disciples that he would send the Comforter, the Holy Spirit, to be with them always. And in the power of the Holy Spirit they did amazing things. Gone was their fear and weakness.

It is perhaps inevitable that we feel unworthy of God's call, and unequal to the work he gives us; but God is not put off by this show of humility, however genuine! He asks, in effect, 'Will you let me make you able to do this?' If we can say 'yes' to that, he will be all our sufficiency, and we shall have nothing to fear. If we venture into a work unasked, we may then expect to fail. But when God sends labourers into his harvest, he never leaves them ill-equipped. We who obey will lack nothing we need for the service of God.

## NO COMPROMISE

*Be patient with everyone. Be kind to each other and to everyone else. Be joyful always. Pray continually. Give thanks in all circumstances. Test everything. Avoid every kind of evil.*
1 THESSALONIANS 5:14–18

D o you notice how positive and challenging these words are? They stress that the Christian way is truly to deny oneself and take up one's cross and follow Jesus. Note: ALL, EVERYONE, ALWAYS, CONTINUALLY—uncompromising words, which should shame the lukewarm Christian. The apostle Paul ends this passage with a prayer which we can echo—that God himself will sanctify us through and through, and that our whole spirit, soul and body may be kept blameless. Again, such definite words. Our God does not do things by halves!

## LIFE'S RICH TAPESTRY

*And we know that in all things God works for the good of those who love him, who have been called according to his purpose.*
ROMANS 8:28

F or a Christian, the Lord Jesus and the threads of life are the warp and weft, which, under God's direction, form a fabric of his designing. The warp is sure, unchangeable, set for the perfect design; the Christian's part is to seek God's guidance for every thread that is to be woven in to complete his pattern. Even our mistakes God will cause to be included, and he will balance the colours and the textures so that it will bring glory to him, the divine Craftsman.

Here we see the meaning of the apostle Paul's words: 'In all things God works for the good of those who love him' (Romans 8:28). He can bring harmony out of discord, good out of apparent disaster, beauty out of the mess we make of our lives.

The cross of crucifixion is ugly in the extreme; yet, in the purpose of God in achieving the work of redemption, it was a thing of majesty. It became a rich tapestry of unbelievable beauty—the meeting point of our sin, and his perfect goodness. And it became the means of salvation and blessing to all mankind.

## LOST DONKEYS—A SURPRISING OUTCOME— 1 SAMUEL 9

*Now the day before Saul came, the* LORD *had revealed this to Samuel: 'About this time tomorrow I will send you a man from the land of Benjamin. Anoint him leader over my people Israel; he will deliver my people from the hand of the Philistines. I have looked upon my people, for their cry has reached me.'*

1 SAMUEL 9:15–16

The first book of Samuel is full of the wonderful working of God in people's lives. In this chapter, a man named Kish has lost his donkeys. He sends his son, Saul, to the hill country to look for them. Little does he realise that Saul will return not only with the donkeys, but having been anointed by Samuel as king over his people!

God works in our own lives, too—often in amazing ways. He can see where we cannot, and to trust him is the only answer to our seemingly insuperable troubles.

When we lose something—or someone—dear to us, we can expect that God has in store an even greater blessing. It may be hard to believe this at the time, but we have a great God. He knows, and he cares.

## THE JEALOUS BROTHER—LUKE 15:28–32

*But we had to celebrate and be glad, because this brother of yours was dead and is alive again; he was lost and is found.*

LUKE 15:32

In the story we know as 'The Prodigal Son', we might have expected the elder brother to have understood his father's feelings about the erring son's return, and even rejoiced with him. The elder son had shared his father's work, home and security; but he had evidently not tried to share his father's burden over the younger son.

What can we learn about ourselves in this? Are we sometimes jealous, even of our brothers and sisters in Christ—jealous of their stronger faith, their joy, their position in the church? Do we sometimes have a little surge of superiority when we know they have failed or shown some sign of weakness, making us feel better about ourselves by contrast? Love—Christian love—does not rejoice over another's failings.

There is surely something lacking in our relationship with Christ if we do not share his grief over our sin, or weakness in another, especially within the family of God. Christians have the wonderful privilege of sharing in the life of our Lord. He showers gifts upon us, supports us with all we need. We can rejoice day by day in his loving presence. If these gifts are given to those weaker than ourselves, or to one who has wronged us, are we going to display jealousy and resentment, or will we rejoice with our Lord over that person?

All true Christians will surely desire always that good should triumph over evil, because they share in the love of the Lord who died to save sinners. And may we never forget that we are accepted by our Heavenly Father, not because of our achievements, but solely by the merits of his Son and his love for us in Jesus Christ.

## TREASURE

*This night your life will be demanded from you. Then who will get what you have prepared for yourself? This is how it will be with anyone who stores up things for himself but is not rich towards God.*

LUKE 12:20–21

This is God speaking to a man who has foolishly stored up an over-abundance of goods for himself alone.

There are two choices we can make: treasure for ourselves, or riches for God. If we are Christians, we will aim to live wholly 'towards God'. All that we say, do and think will be guided to this end. Anything contrary to this will be ruled out.

All day and every day we will be building up treasure of some sort, either earthly or heavenly. Our money or possessions can be used for ourselves—adding to our earthly treasure; or they can be shared with others or used in God's work—adding to our heavenly treasure. The gifts of time, health and strength can all be spent on ourselves or on others.

Earthly—worldly—treasure will perish, a transient pleasure only; pleasing God will bring us true joy and eternal treasure.


## ON ACTIVE SERVICE

*I have no greater joy than to hear that my children are walking in the truth ... We ought therefore to show hospitality to such men so that we may work together for the truth.*

3 JOHN 4, 8

In his third letter, John uses these two expressions: I have no greater joy than to hear that my children are walking in the truth ... that we may work together for the truth.

It is not enough to have discovered the truth—we are to *walk* in the truth. No static condition is this, no being complacent in the knowledge that we are saved through our faith in Christ.

The whole of the New Testament underlines the fact that the life of a Christian is to be one of active obedience—a life of forward movement, progress, growth in spiritual stature. There will be no room for pride, for the Lord is always leading us on to greater endeavour, to greater holiness. As soon as we think we have conquered some particular sin or weakness, he shows us another. (Have you ever climbed a mountain and kept thinking you were near the top, only to find a downward slope hiding another rise?)

John gives us a picture of active service. We cannot sit around in the private office of our lives following the progress of Christ's war against sin, noting the danger spots and waiting for the 'General' to do something about it. No, we are to be actively engaged in the warfare, not simply observers. And we are to be volunteers, not conscripts—willing workers for the truth. This is to be a full-time commitment for life, for there will never be a time on this sin-ridden earth when there are no battles to fight for our Lord.

## BROKEN NETS?—JOHN 21:1–14

*He said, 'Throw your net on the right side of the boat and you will find some.' When they did, they were unable to haul the net in because of the large number of fish.*
JOHN 21:6

Jesus has been crucified. The despondent disciples have gone fishing, and have caught nothing. The risen Jesus appears and tells them to cast the net again—and, behold! Where it had been empty and useless, now it is bearing a mighty catch! Yet it is not broken, as the men would normally expect.

What does this say to us? As disciples of Jesus, we are often empty and useless. At other times we are busily active in the Lord's work, seeming to reap a rich harvest. Sometimes we are too busy, and we break under the strain. If we are empty, it may be because we have not offered ourselves in the Lord's service. If we break, it may well be that the work we undertook was not what he directed us to do; we took matters into our own hands and therefore lacked his strength for the task.

Jesus calls all his disciples to be 'fishers of men'. We are indeed his nets, to be let down at his command. Let us make sure that we go into action only as he wills, and that we act in obedience to him. Then we can be sure that he will give us all the strength we need; we shall not be broken in his service—not, that is, until that day when we are worn out and it is his good pleasure to take us out of service.

## NO ENTRY—MATTHEW 7:15–23

*Not everyone who says to me, 'Lord, Lord,' will enter the kingdom of heaven, but only he who does the will of my Father who is in heaven.*
MATTHEW 7:21

These are hard words, but Jesus knew that some were claiming to act in his name while their hearts were evil. He would not acknowledge these as his followers.

We can call Jesus 'Lord' only if he is indeed the enthroned king in our hearts. When he is truly King and Lord, we shall desire always to know and to do his will. Many people do indeed live good lives which accord with Christ's teaching to some extent; but if they are doing so without truly acknowledging him in their hearts, then they are not recognised as his disciples.

Our Lord makes it clear that outward appearance is irrelevant, and even misleading—'a wolf in sheep's clothing' (verse 15). We find the same idea in 1 Samuel 16:7: 'Man looks at the outward appearance, but the LORD looks at the heart.'

## RIGHT OR WRONG?
*Each of us will give an account of himself to God.*
ROMANS 14:12

In this whole chapter, the apostle Paul is saying, in effect, that if in our hearts we believe a certain thing to be wrong, then we sin by doing it—even if, in fact, we are mistaken in that belief. 'If in doubt, don't!' is good advice.

Paul is concerned with those whose faith is weaker than our own. What is perfectly reconcilable with our own faith may still be wrong if it leads a weaker Christian into sin. Our duty, then, will be to abstain from that action.

Often, something that appears to us harmless can escalate into something harmful—the relating of a funny story, airing a criticism of another person, an acceptable personal indulgence or occupation, and so on. All these may lead a weak person astray. May the Lord help us to be discerning so that we are not stumbling blocks to other Christians.

## TOO MUCH LUGGAGE!

*Enter through the narrow gate. For wide is the gate and broad is the road that leads to destruction, and many enter through it. But small is the gate and narrow the road that leads to life, and only a few find it.*

MATTHEW 7:13–14

*It is easier for a camel to go through the eye of a needle than for a rich man to enter the kingdom of God.*

MATTHEW 19:24

Some have pictured the narrow gate as the little doorway within the big city gate. A camel loaded with goods would not be able to get through.

This is an apt illustration of entry into the kingdom of God. We cannot squeeze through the gate while encumbered with worldly things, or with burdens that we are unwilling to shed, even if we find it in the first place. If, with God's help, we unload our earthly treasures and burdens at the gate, we will find ourselves in company with Jesus—the one who will always bear our burdens with us, and who will shower heavenly gifts upon us.

The way will be Jesus Christ himself (John 14:6). He will lead us to life at its fullest and richest—and he will be our fellow traveller on the whole journey.

## PARADOXES

*Then he called the crowd to him along with his disciples and said: 'If anyone would come after me, he must deny himself and take up his cross and follow me.'*

Mark 8:34

The Christian life is full of paradoxes. Consider these:

We have to put self to death, yet we are promised life to the full with Christ;

We stand alone in our faith and principles amongst unbelievers, yet our Lord is always with us;

We suffer for the sake of Christ, yet we have joy and peace.

One thing is certain—the gains will always outweigh the losses when we follow Christ.


## SPIRITUAL RICHES

*I always thank God for you because of his grace given you in Christ Jesus. For in him you have been enriched in every way ... You do not lack any spiritual gift ...*

1 Corinthians 1:4–7

It is encouraging to note Paul's words 'every' and 'any'. In Christ we are enriched in every way. Do we feel that? We do not lack any spiritual gift. Are we content with too little?

Perhaps, when it comes to gifts of the Spirit, we think it is a case of 'either/or'. But Paul seems to indicate that whatever spiritual gift we need will be given to us for God's service. How reassuring this is!

## SPIRITUAL SURGERY

*I did not come to bring peace, but a sword.*

MATTHEW 10:34–39

These words of Jesus, and the words that follow, make uncomfortable reading. Jesus did not come as a palliative to the consciences of the unrighteous and to give a pat on the back to the apparently righteous. He had work to do—important work that needed a sword.

God, in Christ, had to perform a divine operation, and a painful one, upon man's soul. In everyone who desired God's gift of everlasting life and true peace, there had to be an incision—a cutting away of sin and of dependence upon life's transitory pleasures and selfish ambition.

Only the Divine Surgeon had the wisdom to know what to leave or take away or rearrange. People who thought they could follow Christ and enter his kingdom without radical changes in their lives were much mistaken. Even families would be divided by the 'sword of the Spirit'.

We cannot imagine that Christ would find this process easy; but he knew that those who followed him would, like himself, be despised and rejected, even by their own kith and kin. Their first loyalty was to be to him, and they needed to be prepared for costly warfare.

This is the same for us, today, if we are to enter the kingdom of heaven. Drastic measures may be needed for our salvation. But our hope is in the promise of the Lord Jesus in verse 39: 'Whoever loses his life for my sake will find it.'

## FEARLESS?

*Do not be afraid, just believe.*

MARK 5:36

Jesus says these words; but over and over in the Bible we read of God saying, 'Do not be afraid.' He does not say that we are to try not to worry, or that we are just to do what our feeble strength enables us to do.

Some of us feel that we cannot help worrying—we are, we think, naturally apprehensive types. But the words often used in the Bible are very often commands: 'Be strong!' 'Be courageous!' 'Be not afraid!' If we do not obey, it means we are doubting God's promises.

Do we believe that Jesus Christ is Lord? If we do, we cannot ignore his commands or his promises. It is entirely consistent with all the life and teaching of God in Christ that what he requires of us, he gives power to achieve. He tells us not to be afraid, and to be strong, because he has promised that he himself will be our strength and our peace.

## TWO SIDES OF THE COIN

*I will deliver you, and you will honour me.*

PSALM 50:15

Here we have two complementary statements: God helps; we serve God. It is clear from God's Word that God's action on our behalf is not primarily for our own benefit, certainly not in this life. It is that we may be caught up in the deepest relationship with God—that relationship of service, praise and adoration for which we were created. We are saved in order to serve and to honour God.

## HIDDEN PURPOSES—GENESIS 37:12–28 AND MATTHEW 26:14–16

*Then one of the Twelve—the one called Judas Iscariot—went to the chief priests and asked, 'What are you willing to give me if I hand him over to you?' So they counted out for him thirty silver coins. From then on Judas watched for an opportunity to hand him over.*

MATTHEW 26:14–16

We read in these passages (1) that Joseph's brothers sold him as a slave for twenty pieces of silver, and (2) that, much later, Judas 'sold' Jesus for thirty pieces of silver.

The remarkable thing is that God allowed these events in order to achieve his much greater purposes. Both stories bear witness to God's marvellous overruling of man's evil intent.

In the Genesis account, Jacob, the father, could not know the consequences when he sent his son, Joseph, to his brothers tending the sheep, but he was unwittingly part of the plan. The brothers did what they knew to be wrong, but God used their sin to bring about good. Genesis 50:20 makes it clear: 'You intended to harm me, but God intended it for good to accomplish what is now being done, the saving of many lives.' God the Father knew, of course, what he was doing when he sent his Son into the world. This was to achieve an incomparably greater purpose—the salvation of mankind. Judas, like Joseph's brothers, wilfully sinned, but his sin was used for God's good purposes.

Both these instances are encouraging for us today, and there are lessons to be learned from them. One thing is clear: God can, and does, use our thoughtlessness, and even our deliberate sin, as a master weaver makes faulty strands and mistakes into part of a whole pattern. But we do well to heed our Lord's words in Matthew 26:24: 'Woe to that man who betrays the Son of Man. It would be better for him if he had not been born.' Strong words! Whether we err knowingly or unknowingly, God can, in his mercy and grace, wonderfully use our mistakes. But wilful sin can never be condoned, for God is a righteous Judge.

## GLORY TO GOD

*'I cannot do it,' Joseph replied to Pharaoh, 'but God will give Pharaoh the answer he desires.'*
GENESIS 41:16

Pharaoh had said to Joseph, concerning a dream he had, 'You can interpret it.' Joseph could have taken the credit for doing so; but we see the God-centredness of a truly humble servant: 'I cannot do it ... but God will ...' A true servant of God will always seek to use every opportunity to turn the eyes of unbelievers towards God, that he may be glorified.

Without God, we are nothing. All power belongs to him. As we look at him more and more, and come to know him better, two things are sure to follow: we shall become more genuinely humble, knowing that any good in us is of God; we shall desire increasingly that God be glorified in all things—'Not I, but Christ', as the apostle Paul said.

As Christians, we shall find many opportunities of pointing away from ourselves to God. As Joseph forgave his brothers, he made a memorable statement: 'You meant it for ill, but God meant it for good.' (See Genesis 50:20.) May God help us to witness faithfully in all we do and all we are.

## A SMALL MAN MEETS JESUS—LUKE 19:1–10

*Jesus said to him, 'Today salvation has come to this house, because this man, too, is a son of Abraham. For the Son of Man came to seek and to save what was lost.'*

Luke 19:9–10

We are not told in this passage that Zacchaeus, after his amazing encounter with Jesus, left his home and work to follow him, or even that he was baptised. But we do know that he repented of his sin, his greedy heart was transformed, and he and his household were saved.

This is so with others whose lives were touched by Jesus, and it is the same for many today. Jesus does not call everyone to leave all and follow him into full-time ministry; but he does call everyone to repentance, forgiveness and faith, and to lead godly lives which reflect his own.

Did Zacchaeus perhaps reorganise his team of tax-collectors and inspire a new honesty in them; and perhaps, seeing this, did others come to believe in Jesus? If so, this would be a happy outcome indeed!

## A DEAD MAN LIVES—JOHN 11

*When he heard this, Jesus said, 'This sickness will not end in death. No, it is for God's glory so that God's Son may be glorified through it.'*

John 11:4

Did Jesus delay going to Lazarus because he knew that, by God's power, the dead man's body had been kept from decay? Or did he know his power to restore dead and decaying flesh and organs? Or was it, as Jesus said, purely that a greater miracle could be performed for the glory of God, and to strengthen people's belief in him?

Mary and Martha were tested to the limit in this episode, with their total incomprehension of the behaviour of Jesus, and of his intention. Two days had passed since they had sent their message telling Jesus that their brother was sick. Can we hear the voice of suffering humanity through all the ages in this?

This miracle was not something to be done in secret, but was of such importance that Jesus intended maximum publicity. Why did Jesus weep, since he knew what he was about to do? He would, of course, be moved by the grief of his friends. It could also have been a deep agonising over the world's unbelief. In all this, there are points which may help us:

Jesus teaches us that it is not always right—for us, or for God himself—to leap into action. More can sometimes be achieved by leaving the situation for a while, praying and considering. And if God delays in answering our prayers, it will be because he knows it is all right!

Jesus allowed the two sisters to suffer grief in order to accomplish something of eternal significance. Our earthly trials are small in the light of God's eternal purposes. Jesus gave thanks before the miracle took place. Can we do this in our prayers?

Others had to take the stone from the tomb; but we, like Lazarus, have to come out of our 'tomb' when Jesus calls, and so become free.

## A SPRING OF WATER

*The water I give … will become … a spring of water welling up to eternal life.*

JOHN 4:14

A Christian's life is not to be a stagnant pool, but a 'spring of water welling up'. Jesus is referring to the water that he offers us, and it will be for eternal life. There is to be constant movement, ceaseless flowing of water from its source. It is free-flowing power and life coming from God the Father, and issuing forth from us.

There is to be a continual refreshing and purifying in the Christian's life. This is possible only if the channel is kept unclogged. Then the power of God the Holy Spirit will be poured out from us.

Spring water is pure because it is free flowing, continually moving. That is its value. A stagnant pool is inviting to no one; nor is a stagnant Christian life.


## GOD LOVES ME!

*Whoever has my commands and obeys them, he is the one who loves me. He who loves me will be loved by my Father, and I too will love him …*

JOHN 14:21


Jesus makes it clear that love between him and ourselves is mutual, and requires our obedience. Some people cannot grasp that God loves each of us personally. Yes, we may feel unlovable and unworthy; but here we have a personal assurance from Jesus. Do we love him, and seek to obey him (even if we often fail)? Then he loves each one of us. He loves you and he loves me. What is more, he and the Father will make their home in us (John 14:23). Such thoughts are wonderful beyond comprehension.

## PEACE

*Therefore, since we have been justified through faith, we have peace with God through our Lord Jesus Christ ... .*
ROMANS 5:1

The apostle Paul does not say we can expect peace some time in the future, or that we may perhaps have peace sometimes, or that, if all goes well, we shall have peace. He says, with certainty, 'We have peace.' It is not promised only to the few who lack adversity. He does not say we shall have peace except when we have a headache or backache, or except when circumstances are particularly trying. There is only one condition: justification through faith—we must be right with God. Are we meeting that criterion, believing and trusting in the Lord Jesus to rescue us from sin? If so, we have peace, now, regardless of our present situation.

Peace in the midst of strife? Yes. The issue is already known, the final victory won. Certainly, there are 'mopping-up tactics' to be dealt with after every battle. But nothing can alter the fact that ours is the victory in Christ, who has already conquered sin and death.


## LIVING TREES

*Blessed is the man who trusts in the Lord, whose confidence is in him. He will be like a tree planted by the water, that sends out its roots by the stream. It does not fear when heat comes; its leaves are always green. It has no worries in time of drought and never fails to bear fruit.*
JEREMIAH 17:7–8

This is a beautiful and inspiring passage, for Jesus Christ himself is the Living Water. When we are firmly established beside him—and in him—we will always be able to bear fruit for him.

Whatever the circumstances—in the heat of battle with Satan or with our own problems, in times of dryness or hardship, even in old age—we need not fear. We cannot escape difficulties, sorrow, disappointment or ill health, and during these times we may feel dry and withered. But we always have the Living Water to draw upon—Jesus has promised to be with us always.

So let us send out our roots, draw deeply from the written Word (see Psalm 1) which speaks so wonderfully of him who is the Living Word—Jesus himself. Thus we will find strength to stand, grow and bear fruit.

## GOD-CENTRED PRAYER—2 SAMUEL 7:18–29

*How great you are, O Sovereign LORD! There is no one like you, and there is no God but you, as we have heard with our own ears.*
2 SAMUEL 7:22

Within these verses is a wonderful pattern for prayer: You know your servant, Lord. How great you are. There is no one like you, and there is no God but you. Lord God, keep for ever the promise you have made. Do as you promised, so that your name will be great for ever. O Sovereign LORD, you are God! Your words are trustworthy. Now be pleased to bless us, for you have spoken.

This is God-centred prayer. To base our prayer on God's promises and upon his revealed word will ensure that we pray with thankfulness, confidence and praise. Such prayer is surely pleasing to God, and it will bring us closer to him.

## WORSHIP IN ADVERSITY—PSALM 119:65–72

*It was good for me to be afflicted so that I might learn your decrees.*

PSALM 119:71

Sometimes it is the evidence of God's activity in adversity that moves us to worship, more so even than when we are contemplating beauty in his creation. Many people who take the good things of life for granted fail to meet with God until they experience trouble. Possibly their first real experience of him is when they turn to him in desperation and find their deepest needs met in his wonderful way.

In Psalm 119:71, the writer says an amazing thing: 'It was good for me to be afflicted so that I might learn your decrees.' Many of us may feelingly echo that statement, realising that it is worth absolutely anything to have a true experience of God.

The focal point of Christian worship is an instrument of cruel torture—a cross of crucifixion. The cross of Christ is the evidence that God is at work, meeting people's need. It is a symbol of his love for us in delivering us from sin and death. We worship and praise him for his wonderful gift.

### FREE!

*Blessed is he whose help is the God of Jacob, whose hope is in the LORD his God, the Maker of heaven and earth, the sea, and everything in them—the LORD, who remains faithful for ever. He upholds the cause of the oppressed and gives food to the hungry. The LORD sets prisoners free…*

PSALM 146:5–7

God means us to be free. This is clear from the number of references in the Bible. Here is a small selection for us to ponder: God promises to 'free captives from prison and to release from the dungeon those who sit in darkness' (Isaiah 42:7). This freedom is from spiritual and moral bondage for the captives in Babylon.

'The LORD sets prisoners free.' (Psalm 146:7) These prisoners are God's oppressed people everywhere.

'I run in the paths of your commands, for you have set my heart free.' (Psalm 119:32)

Jesus says, 'If the Son sets you free, you will be free indeed.' (John 8:36)

Are we imprisoned by fear? The Lord has said, 'Don't be afraid.' (Matthew 10:31)

Are we trapped in a web of anxiety? The Lord has said, 'Do not worry.' (Matthew 6:31)

Are we fettered by insecurity? The Lord has promised that if we seek first the kingdom of God, he will supply all our needs. (Matthew 6:33)

Are we bound by some particular sin? In Christ we have victory over sin. (1 Corinthians 15:57)

In everything, our Lord is a wonderful deliverer!


## FIT FOR SERVICE—THOUGHTS FROM ISAIAH 6:1–8

*'Woe to me …for I am a man of unclean lips …'*
*'Your guilt is taken away and your sin atoned for.'*
ISAIAH 6:5–6


God desires to cleanse us from our sin. We cannot serve him until we are cleansed by him, and he wants our service. We are not, then, asking a favour when we seek God's forgiveness; we are asking that which he intends in the gospel of his grace. It is he who has put into our hearts that need of forgiveness that we bring to him, but he does require true repentance. When we are aware of God, we feel a sense of awe, of worship. In his light we recognise our sin and unworthiness. The Lord Jesus offers to cleanse us by his blood shed for us on the cross, and God sent him for just that. Our forgiveness is necessary for our service.

## ABUNDANT LIFE

*I have come that they may have life and have it to the full.*
JOHN 10:10

Jesus still speaks these words to us today. How mistaken we are if we think that following Christ means denial of everything we enjoy! Yes, some things may have to go, but consider how much he gives—more than we can ask or think or deserve. He gives his presence to be with us always and everywhere; his joy as we grow in understanding of him; his love for us, and our desire to love others; his peace; his guidance; the power of his Holy Spirit to uphold us and enable us to serve him—and, at the end, eternal life in his presence.

Numberless blessings ensure that we shall have life to the full—abundant life. The most wonderful thing is that the more we ourselves give, the more we receive—sometimes worldly gifts, and certainly 'heavenly' treasure. Thanks be to God!

## DO IT YOURSELF!

*My people have committed two sins: They have forsaken me, the spring of living water, and have dug their own cisterns, broken cisterns that cannot hold water.*

JEREMIAH 2:13

Many of us put our trust in 'broken cisterns' of some kind. It may be that we rely on others too much, or that we aim for more and more possessions or success, or indulge our bodies to our own hurt. We think that, in such ways, we can store up happiness and security for ourselves. But, just as water inevitably seeps away from a broken tank, so we, in our misjudged agenda, may find ourselves increasingly empty. We may not notice this until the 'water' on which we set such store suddenly gushes out, leaving us drained and helpless. It may happen so gradually that we fail to notice what is happening.

Only in the Lord Jesus can we safely put our trust. He is to us a well of water—living water that will wholly satisfy our thirst, water that will never fail because there is no flaw in the well.

The sooner we scrap our homemade 'cisterns', the better, for they will not last. Then we can commit ourselves entirely to God, the Living Water, by faith in Jesus. We will not only satisfy our own thirst—others may be led to drink, too.

## A LOOK AT THE PROPHET JEREMIAH

*The word of the* Lord *came to me, saying, 'Before I formed you in the womb I knew you, before you were born I set you apart; I appointed you as a prophet to the nations.'*
Jeremiah 1:4–5

Jeremiah had a message of hope and comfort to declare, but it was an unpopular message because it was conditional. It required a change of heart in the people, and they did not want that.

God's word is always challenging, although it offers salvation and hope. So, in every age, it has been rejected by a great many people. In every age, God's faithful messengers have been persecuted as they proclaimed it—Jeremiah, the apostle Paul, our Lord Jesus himself, and many, many others.

These had a far wider audience than most of us will have, but we are not absolved from our responsibilities. Every Christian is expected to witness before others and, like Jeremiah at the beginning, we may well shrink from the task, even when it may only involve risking a little unpopularity.

Are we faithful in proclaiming and living out the truth amongst those with whom we work, or in our families and our circle of friends, or do we keep quiet, convincing ourselves that we have no right to impose our views on other people?

Consider what Jeremiah suffered through his faithfulness in proclaiming God's word: He became to others a man of strife and contention, and he had to bear their curses, though he was blameless in his life; he had to endure slander; he was beaten and put in the stocks, but still he said, 'Thus says the Lord ...'; he was mocked, but still he was compelled in his heart to speak out for

God; he was threatened with death at the hands of the priests and prophets, but he knew that the word and the will of God could not be denied; he was imprisoned more than once, on one occasion being thrown into a filthy cistern.

Does all this make us feel shamefully feeble in our witness? Maybe God does not call you and me to such a great and daring mission. But Jesus did command us, his disciples, to proclaim the gospel. Oh, that we might fearlessly do this, and, in humility, bear with grace all that befalls us as a result! We always go in the strength of the Lord. We do not need anything more.


## S O S FROM THE WORLD—PSALM 12

*Help, LORD, for the godly are no more.*
PSALM 12:1

The whole of Psalm 12 is an outcry against the wicked, when 'vileness is honoured'. It is a cry from the heart for the Lord God to take action.

Is it any different today? In our world, unlawful sex, crime and violence are exalted in all their evil in books, plays, art and the media; we cannot escape from it. For the psalmist, the manifestation of sin may have been different in many ways; but we, today, share his grief at the 'oppression of the weak and the groaning of the needy'. War and injustice will always be with us, it seems.

To God, the earth must appear as a great festering sore—as indeed it looks to us. Everyone is infected to some degree. What does this mean to our Heavenly Father as he looks upon this spoiling of his beautiful world? Were it not for his tremendous, unfathomable love for his people, he would surely wash his hands of us. But the Lord Jesus has come. He, and he only, can arrest, even cure, the disease of sin—and this he does in the glorious outworking of the gospel of his grace.

How wonderful it will be when sin and ugliness are no more and we are caught up into God's presence! We shall see his beauty, and be 'transported in wonder and praise'.

## EXTRAS

*God ... richly provides us with everything for our enjoyment.*
1 TIMOTHY 6:17

Sometimes we feel guilty about actually enjoying the good things in life—things that are over and above our daily requirements of food, clothing and warmth. But if these were all that God intended us to have, he could have made the world in black and white! Why bother with varied colours, or fragrances or anything beautiful? Clearly, God knew that we needed beauty and colour to balance the necessities of life—and how we praise him for that!

## GOD'S PERSPECTIVE—1 THESSALONIANS CHAPTERS 1 AND 2

*For we know, brothers loved by God, that he has chosen you, because our gospel came to you not simply with words, but also with power, with the Holy Spirit and with deep conviction. You know how we lived among you for your sake. You became imitators of us and of the Lord; in spite of severe suffering, you welcomed the message with the joy given by the Holy Spirit.*
1 THESSALONIANS 1:4–6

In these two chapters, the apostle Paul clearly sets life in God's perspective: he has chosen us; he calls us; we aim to please God, not others; we are to live lives worthy of God; we are not to look for praise from people.

God is the beginning and end of our whole life. He created and chose us, and it is he who calls us to live for him. The driving force of our life is from God. The purpose of our life is to please God. The end of our life is to return to God. How we stand in the eyes of the world is unimportant—except in so far as we can, by our witness, bring glory to God.

This temporal body is only an earthen vessel to contain the Spirit, or a channel for the free flowing of God's love and power and truth to as many people as we can reach.

How we fuss and fret about so many things in our worldly circumstances! If only we could see these in God's eternal perspective, we might concentrate on the one essential—to glorify God in all things.

## JUST AS I AM

*Shall what is formed say to him who formed it, 'Why did you make me like this?'*

ROMANS 9:20

How can we expect or hope to fathom the depths of God's purposes for us and for the gospel? He created us with human potentialities and with limitations, and we shall always remain created things, dependent for everything upon our Maker. Everything we need is supplied by him. Even man-made fibres depend on his provision of the raw materials, and on the power given to us to make use of these things. We are in no position to question or challenge God. Neither can we ever glory in ourselves, since it is God who works in us. It is God's right to do with us just as he may be pleased.

## A QUIET LIFE

*Aspire to live quietly.*

1 Thessalonians 4:11 (Authorised Version)

Do you rush around trying to do too much, wearing yourself out? Most of us do. Especially, we may worry that there is not enough time for the really important things, such as helping the needy people around us. But if we stay close to the Lord, he will make known to us his will for each day. He knows our limitations, and he will require of us only what we are able to do in his strength, as well as what he considers necessary for us to do. When we realise this, we can go forward in quietness and confidence.

If we ourselves feel the pressure of so much to be done, so many people to help, imagine how much more Jesus could have felt it— crowds waiting for healing, needing his teaching and his help. He had such a short time for such tremendous work—how could he ever achieve it? But what do we find? He moved about doing his work quietly—no panic, no nervous exhaustion. Physical tiredness, yes; and he would often go alone to a quiet place to speak with his Father. Sometimes he spoke to crowds, sometimes only to a few; but whatever he was doing, he dealt patiently with any interruptions that occurred, and gave his attention to the need of the moment.

We can learn so much from this. God knows which lives we are to touch, which tasks are truly important in his sight. Jesus spent much time with only his twelve disciples in spite of the thronging crowds wanting his attention, and what fruit that has borne! So let us walk quietly with him who will direct our steps and cause us to bring forth fruit to his glory.

## A LOOK AT JUDAS

*Man looks at the outward appearance, but the LORD looks at the heart.*

1 SAMUEL 16:7

In John 13:21–30, we have the tragic story of the betrayal of Jesus by Judas.

Evidently, Judas appeared to be a loyal disciple like the other eleven. When Jesus says that one of them will betray him, they seem perplexed, even doubting their own allegiance—'Is it I?' But Jesus discerns the intention of Judas—he looks not at the outward appearance, but at the heart—and knows he is the betrayer.

We have already been given a glimpse of Judas' worldliness when he complains about Mary's extravagance with the precious ointment poured out on Jesus' feet—though his main criticism seemed to be that it could have been sold for charitable purposes. We know, too, that he was the treasurer for the group, and a dishonest one. There are indications of worldliness in the other disciples, too. None was perfect, and perhaps Judas appeared no worse than they were.

How treacherous are the hearts of men and women. Even today, many people make an outward show of Christian discipleship while bearing in their hearts selfish motives, wrong desires or the worship of 'idols' of one kind or another. Their inward being is well disguised, but the Lord looks into each heart and knows who are his.

When we have failed the Lord, he desires to forgive, not condemn. By his grace, we may return to him and find forgiveness, acceptance and love.

## PRAYER BEFORE ACTION

*Hear us, O our God, for we are despised … They have thrown insults in the face of the builders. So we rebuilt the wall.*
NEHEMIAH 4:4–6

The Jewish exiles had been allowed to return to Jerusalem to rebuild its wall, but they were coming up against opposition and insults. So Nehemiah prayed—and the work began again!

When we have prayed for God's help and protection, we do not sit back and leave the work to him; we take God-guided action. It may mean working 'with our weapon in one hand' (Nehemiah 4:17), and being watchful and prepared to use it—Satan's opposition is real when God's work is going forward.

In our work for the Lord, we need to be equally watchful of our own motives and feelings, putting to death self-consciousness, feeble-heartedness or pride. It may mean risking unpopularity by taking a firm stand on some issue. It will certainly mean guarding against discouragement and despair.

Someone has said, 'Nehemiah got the balance right: he watched as if it all depended on him, and prayed as if it all depended on God.'

## DRESSING UP

*Clothe yourselves with the Lord Jesus Christ.*

ROMANS 13:14

The apostle Paul is giving this advice as an alternative to gratifying 'the desires of the sinful nature', to which he has previously referred, and which we are to 'put aside'. This is to say that we are not to indulge ourselves with this world's pleasures.

Think of children dressing up. When they put on different clothes for a fancy-dress party, or simply put on grown-up clothing as a pretence, they do not just resemble the assumed characters—they behave like them. In a sense, they become the part, taking on the emotions and characteristics of the one they believe themselves to be.

So Paul's words are apt: to clothe ourselves with the Lord Jesus Christ is actually to become more like him—not in appearance, but in our whole nature. We will share his mind, his feelings, his communicable attributes. This is important, for only as we are clothed with him in his righteousness can we approach our holy God.


## RIGHT PRIORITIES—NEHEMIAH CHAPTERS 8 AND 9

*Ezra opened the book. All the people could see him because he was standing above them; and as he opened it, the people all stood up. Ezra praised the* LORD, *the great God; and all the people lifted their hands and responded, 'Amen! Amen!' Then they bowed down and worshiped the* LORD *with their faces to the ground.*

NEHEMIAH 8:5–6

These chapters have much to teach us. Once the wall of Jerusalem had been built, and whole families had returned to inhabit the city and towns round about, they were all called together to hear the Word of God—the Book of the Law of Moses. They came penitently before God, confessing their own sin, as well as the iniquities of their ancestors. These actions led to a time of praise and worship as God's attributes were highlighted: his graciousness and mercy, his patience, his steadfast love, his understanding.

What a wonderful pattern to follow! The sequence, repeated over and over, amongst God's people today is: blessing—rebellion—chastening—repentance—restoration. And after restoration there is rejoicing (as in chapter 12:43)—rejoicing which could be heard far away.

How often does the sound of rejoicing from the church reach people far away?

## CARRY ME!

*Save your people and bless your inheritance; be their shepherd and carry them for ever.*

PSALM 28:9

In ordinary life we are expected to stand on our own feet; but in the spiritual realm we are to allow ourselves to be carried. God would have us utterly dependent upon him. It is in that very dependence that our salvation lies. 'But because of his great love for us, God, who is rich in mercy, made us alive with Christ even when we were dead in transgressions—it is by grace you have been saved' (Ephesians 2:4–5).

To allow ourselves to be carried by God, and led by God as the Eastern shepherds lead their sheep, implies that complete trust which is dear to the heart of God. Our admission of the need to be carried in this way is an essential act of submission to him.

## DESPAIR IN THE NIGHT

*I cried out to God for help ... at night I stretched out untiring hands and my soul refused to be comforted.*

PSALM 77:1-2

W ho has not known the negative, dark feelings in long wakeful stretches of the night? The antidote, as we see later in this psalm, is to remember what God has done in the past. There is enough, for most of us, in that to keep us from despair.

Yet, the writer says, 'Your footprints were not seen' (verse 19). God has been doing wonderful things, but the people have failed to recognise his hand in it all. Isn't this true in our own lives? And do we sometimes blame God for ills that befall us, while failing to see him at work in what is good?

So what shall we do in the small hours, awake in bed? The psalmist answers us clearly: 'I will meditate on all your works and consider all your mighty deeds.' *That* might keep us happily awake for the rest of the night!

## GOOD EYESIGHT

*The eye is the lamp of the body. If your eyes are good, your whole body will be full of light.*

MATTHEW 6:22

Jesus is the Light of the World. He is total light for our total darkness. There is no twilight area between God and us. Either we focus our eyes on Christ, drawing his light into ourselves, or we remain in spiritual darkness. In his light we can approach God and be in relationship with him. His light will shine through us to reach the darkness in the people around us. What a wonderful privilege is ours!

## THE GREATER FEAR—MARK 4:35–41

*A furious squall came up, and the waves broke over the boat, so that it was nearly swamped. Jesus was in the stern, sleeping on a cushion. The disciples woke him and said to him, 'Teacher, don't you care if we drown?'*

MARK 4:37–38

Here we read how Jesus, in a boat with his disciples, calmed the sudden storm.

The disciples were afraid they would drown. Jesus, who was sleeping in the boat, was shaken urgently by the men shouting, 'Don't you care?' But they seem to have been even more frightened by Jesus' power over the elements. They were terrified. 'Who is this?' These men had seen Jesus performing miracles, heard him teaching with authority, and witnessed his healing power. But they still did not understand their Master. They are still taken by surprise at his power, and so afraid that they could not even voice their question to Jesus himself.

How would we react to someone in our midst, uniquely, powerfully in charge? Are we not often afraid of what we do not understand, for there are astonishing possibilities? We have an advantage over those first disciples, for we have become familiar, through the Bible, with Jesus' awesome power and authority. Yet we still say, when a prayer is answered directly, 'How extraordinary!' as if we had not really expected God to act. Jesus might well challenge you and me about our faith—or lack of it—as he challenged his disciples. Everything is possible with God and, because we know his love for us, we need never be afraid of what he will do.


## LIFE WORTH LIVING

*For everything God created is good, and nothing is to be rejected if it is received with thanksgiving, because it is consecrated by the word of God and prayer.*
1 TIMOTHY 4:4–5

There is absolutely nothing that is worth anything unless God's blessing is upon it. If it is not pleasing to God, it will bring no lasting satisfaction or fulfilment to the Christian. The teaching of the Bible upholds this. It is a dead thing that is not blessed by God. In the perplexing decisions we have to make, the sure and final test of the rightness of anything is whether we can ask God's blessing on it.

Everything in a Christian's life should in some way add something to his spiritual stature—not for the boosting of his own ego, but for the glory of God. We are 'not our own', but are 'bought with a price' and belong to God (1 Corinthians 6:19–20).

When God formed men and women, breathing into their nostrils the breath of life, they became living souls (Genesis 2:7)—not just animals, living blindly by instinct, but living souls capable of communion with the living God and Creator.

We need to pray constantly that he will fill us with his own Spirit so that we may live worthily for him.


## OUR WONDERFUL GOD

*Lord, you have been our dwelling place throughout all generations. Before the mountains were born or you brought forth the earth and the world, from everlasting to everlasting you are God.*

PSALM 90:1–2

God is eternal—past, present and future.

He has existed always, and will exist for ever.

His promises are being fulfilled all the time; we do not have to wait for them in some distant future.

He is with us all the time in our short life-span; at any time we can turn to him and he is near.

Day and night he is ready to hear our prayers and praise.

In him we have eternal life now, and heaven is all about us now and for all time.


## FROM DESPAIR TO PRAISE—PSALM 28

*The LORD is my strength and my shield; my heart trusts in him,*

*and I am helped. My heart leaps for joy and I will give thanks to*
*him in song.*

PSALM 28:7

There are no doubt many who, like the psalmist, have started to pray on a note of despair, of pleading, and then almost at once found such heartfelt assurance, that the plea is turned to praise.

We perhaps fall on our knees, in tears, desperate for help, guidance, comfort, forgiveness or whatever the need. Then, even as we pour out our need, there is that 'still, small voice'—an awareness that God knows and cares and will act. There is an instant transition from 'Do not turn a deaf ear to me' (verse 1) to 'He has heard' (verse 6); from 'I call to you for help' (verse 2) to 'I am helped' (verse 7).

We start with hands lifted up in supplication, and end with exulting hearts and a song of thanksgiving. We know, deep in our hearts, that we trust him, and that makes all the difference. It is, in fact, the reason why we cried to him in the first place.

## A HOUSE FOR GOD

*Here am I, living in a palace of cedar, while the ark of God*
*remains in a tent.*

2 SAMUEL 7:1–17

We cannot help but admire David's impulse to bring God's dwelling more up to the level of his own—he, David, living in a palace, while God dwelt in a tent? Never! But God does not necessarily value what we value.

As God speaks to Nathan, it becomes clear that by the word 'house', God means something different from David. God is not in need of a house, though the time would come, during Solomon's reign, when he would consent to a house 'made with hands'. This would not be because he must have a shelter, but that, through the gifts and toil of men, God might be remembered, worshipped and glorified. Now, though, God speaks of building David a house (verse 11).

David may live in a palace, but the 'House of David' is yet to be established by God for ever—not a building, but the kingdom of great David's greater Son.

Such a comparison holds good for the church. The true Church is not bricks and mortar, but people—a living, indestructible thing. The Son of God had nowhere to lay his head (Matthew 8:20), yet he says, 'In my Father's house are many rooms' (John 14:2).

He himself dwells there, now and for ever, and in this house he 'prepares a place' for us, so that we may find eternal shelter there. May our earthly home never be such an all-sufficient shelter that we fail to seek him who has been, and is, 'our dwelling place in all generations' (Psalm 90:1).


## WHY SHOULD I LOVE GOD?

*How great is the love the Father has lavished on us, that we should be called children of God! And that is what we are! The reason the world does not know us is that it did not know him.*
1 JOHN 3:1

*This is love: not that we loved God, but that he loved us and sent his Son as an atoning sacrifice for our sins.*
1 JOHN 4:10

When people ask this question, as many do, we need to know the true meaning of the word 'love' as used in the Bible if we are to answer the question.

Love, in the biblical sense, does not often mean spontaneous, emotional love between people. It is, rather, a positive and deliberate act of reaching out to others for their good, regardless of our natural feelings for them.

The finest example, of course, is Jesus Christ, who loved us so much that he was prepared to die a cruel death for us. God, in Christ, has demonstrated his own love.

The love which God requires of us is to be totally willing and selfless. We cannot love with our emotions in response to a command. To love God is a turning towards him and all that he stands for: goodness, truth, light, love itself and all his qualities. It is to recognise him for who he is and to respond to him. God commands our love because he knows that there is no true life apart from him. To love him involves freely placing our will alongside his and living according to his laws.

Does loving and serving God mean denying ourselves all that we naturally desire and want? No. But as we come to know God better, we learn that he never denies except to give something greater—though we may not discover this at once. He is not like an over-indulgent father; in his wisdom and love he sees beyond our immediate wants.

Jesus did say, 'Deny yourself', yes, and we shall, in love, want to do this. But he also said that he had come that we might have life to the full—'more abundant' life (John 10:10). The more we learn of God and the more we discover the blessings he showers upon us, the more we shall come to love and trust him—not in obedience to a command, but as a natural response to him in his love for us.

## GOD IN CONTROL

*The battle is the LORD's, and he will give all of you into our hands.*

1 SAMUEL 17:47

So often this is true for the Christian in the battle against self, sin and the evil in the world. Some of us fuss so much, fearful as we go to meet each day, conscious of our weakness, our proneness to temptation, our diffidence in speaking up for the Lord. It surely should help us to remember that these are the Lord's battles, and we may be fully assured of his help and strength.

Goliath had 'defied the armies of the living God', and this was David's reason for doing battle with this Philistine. The Christian is fired into action for the same reason—to defend the name of the Lord. God always promises his presence and help in such battles.

The Bible is full of examples of God's involvement with us in battle. Just as David had success in all his undertakings 'because the LORD was with him' (1 Samuel 18:14), even so shall we find that God wins battles in and through us—for his name's sake. The battle is Christ's, the strength is Christ's and the victory is Christ's. As long as we remember this, we shall never feel defeated; nor shall we have any cause for pride.


## PRAISE ON A JOURNEY—ECHOES OF PSALM 139

*O LORD, you have searched me and you know me.*
*You know when I sit and when I rise; you perceive my thoughts from afar.*

PSALM 139:1–2

O Lord, you have set this little world in the vastness of the universe. Yet we are not lost on our fragment of it, for you have visited us here in the person of Jesus Christ. You have set your great and kindly providence over us like a canopy, and under us like a cradle, so that we are perpetually enfolded in your tender care.

We are so small and you are so great; yet you became small so that we might become great in you, growing to the full stature of children of God. We are set in the midst of boundless space, but your love is boundless, too, and your presence is all around us.

If we travel to the limits of our country, you are there; if we cross the seas to the other side of the world, you go with us all the way; if we penetrate Africa's darkest jungle, you are even there. We cannot escape from your presence even if we wished it. All the world's distances are only a span of your hand, and everywhere and for ever we can know you near.

Even when we leave this little world and embark on the unknown journey, we can but come closer to you. Glory be to you, O God, and praise and thanksgiving for ever.

## AN EASY BURDEN
*My yoke is easy and my burden is light.*
MATTHEW 11:30

Jesus describes his yoke as easy because he is our strength; the burden is light because he shares it with us.

We can perhaps see a picture in this of a father and his child carrying together a heavy bucket of water. The child is 'helping', but it is the father who has the real strength and who takes the main weight. The child helps to the extent that his strength will allow. If he were to let go, the bucket would not drop!

We do not carry the whole weight in our Christian work; we are 'workers together with God' (1 Corinthians 3:9) and he is the power behind all that work.

## RIGHT TURN

*Turn from your evil ways.*

EZEKIEL 33:11–16

H ere it is stated that it is better to have been evil and then turn to good than to have been good and then turn to evil. Either way, the past can be wiped out. There is either a deliberate, permanent state of repentance, or a deliberate turning away from God.

We know that, when a sinner repents, God forgives. And he casts the remembrance of the sin into the depths of the sea: You will again have compassion on us; you will tread our sins underfoot and hurl all our iniquities into the depths of the sea (Micah 7:19). Thank God for that!

## A WIDER CONTEXT

*Your word, O LORD, is eternal; it stands firm in the heavens. Your faithfulness continues through all generations; you established the earth, and it endures. Your laws endure to this day, for all things serve you.*

PSALM 119:89–91

The vastness of the universe is incredibly wonderful. It is thought that some of the stars we see are travelling away from us all the time, or have already ceased to be! As more and more powerful telescopes are made, even more stars are discovered beyond those already known—more galaxies of millions of stars with their planets!

But here in this limitless universe is a special little gem containing the most amazingly intricate life—plants and animals and, perhaps, most amazing of all, humankind with a soul, and a mind trying to comprehend God, the Creator. How God must love this special, unique, planet! How insane we are when we are bent on destroying, deliberately or in ignorance, this wonder of life instead of enjoying it!

We are, as someone has said, a 'visited planet'. God has been here, walking and talking, touching and being touched—in the person of Jesus Christ. 'The Word became flesh and made his dwelling among us. We have seen his glory, the glory of the One and Only, who came from the Father, full of grace and truth' (John 1:14). Though withdrawn in body now, he is still with us through the Holy Spirit, and has promised to be faithful 'through all generations'.

How we praise you, Creator God!


## ON A JOURNEY

*To God's elect, strangers in the world ...*

I PETER 1:1


We are commuters between heaven and earth. Every day we live in the world, but we make frequent excursions to heaven—in prayer, in worship, in seeking enlightenment and communion with God, in meditation and contemplation.

We need spiritual strength for our earthly existence—and this he gives us day by day as we draw near to him in the reading of his Word, the Bible, and prayer.

## OBEDIENCE AND PROMISE

*I am laid low in the dust; preserve my life according to your word.*
PSALM 119:25

In Psalm 119, the psalmist's cry to God concerns, first, God's word and promise and, second, the psalmist's obedience.

Two phrases keep occurring: 'according to your word' and 'according to your promise'. There is, here, no empty hope. His cry is based on a knowledge of God's faithfulness: 'according to your justice'; 'according to your steadfast love'. The knowledge of God's faithfulness gives hope. We can have this knowledge, too—by reading in the Bible of God's dealings with people, and also from a personal experience of trusting God.

We cannot expect God's help if we ourselves are not faithful, and obedient to that which we know of his will for us. Jesus said, 'If you remain in me and my words remain in you, ask whatever you wish, and it will be given you' (John 15:7) and 'If you obey my commands, you will remain in my love' (John 15:10). And we read in 1 John 2:3: 'We know that we have come to know [Jesus] if we obey his commands.'

Obedience to God and his promises to us are clearly interdependent.

## WHAT GOD MEANS TO US—THOUGHTS ON PSALM 62

*My soul finds rest in God alone; my salvation comes from him.*
*He alone is my rock and my salvation; he is my fortress, I will*
*never be shaken.*

PSALM 62:1–2

He means peace in heart and soul.

He gives help in life and is a firm foundation.

He is strength and protection and security, and he is hope.

He is our salvation and honour, and he is a refuge.

He is at all times to be trusted, and we can tell him all that is in our hearts.

He brings our lives into better perspective, showing us a greater purpose.

He will reward us according to deeds which profess our love for him.

What a God!

## THE WAY OF SALVATION

*'We are punished justly, for we are getting what our deeds*
*deserve. But this man has done nothing wrong ... Jesus,*
*remember me when you come into your kingdom.' Jesus*
*answered him ... 'Today you will be with me in paradise.'*

LUKE 23:41–43

This thief on the cross beside Jesus provides a remarkable picture of the way of salvation:

Acceptance of one's own guilt.

Belief in Christ's sinlessness.

Desire to be accepted into Christ's kingdom.
Acceptance by Christ.

## STILL WAITING—ROMANS 8:18–25

*The creation waits in eager expectation ...*
ROMANS 8:19

This whole passage speaks of incompletion, and of eager expectation. Christians are already sons and daughters of God, but there is more to come. We know that the Holy Spirit lives within us now, but we do not have complete and constant joyfulness—we 'groan inwardly', awaiting the full and 'glorious freedom of the children of God'.

We have not yet arrived. In fact, we have only just started the journey—one which will be difficult, painful, costly at times. We travel with a deep inner joy and hope, yes—but the culmination, the supreme joy, is yet to come.

May we wait patiently, but expectantly, for the full realisation of our inheritance in Christ, the final redemption of our bodies, and the sight of him in his glory.

## PEACE BEYOND UNDERSTANDING

*My peace I give you. I do not give to you as the world gives.*
JOHN 14:27

How can we find peace in this troubled world? There may be brief lulls in conflict, but all is unpredictable. In our own personal world, too, we are at the mercy of our moods and ever-changing circumstances.

What is the special peace that Jesus offers? It is peace that is constant, whatever the situation, because it rests on the fact that God is ultimately in control. God is changeless; Christ has promised to be with us always—not just when things are going well. Our peace rests on those assurances.

The source of Jesus' own peace was the Father's constant presence and declared purpose for him, and his power at work in him. In quiet communion with him, Jesus found the peace and the strength to fulfil that purpose.

This is the peace that Jesus will give us, as we strive to follow him and do his will.

## WHY DO THE WICKED PROSPER?—PSALM 73

*But as for me, my feet had almost slipped; I had nearly lost my foothold. For I envied the arrogant when I saw the prosperity of the wicked.*

PSALM 73:2–3

This is a tricky question and, anyway, is it always the case? We often ask, too, why the 'good' suffer—and we have no easy answer to that.

It may be helpful to consider these alternatives: Which is better—to suffer in this life but have God hold us by the hand, or to possess all in this life and be apart from God? Which is preferable—to have ill-fortune on earth followed by endless peace and rest, or to enjoy good fortune here followed by eternal separation from God?

These are not, of course, mutually exclusive, but there is a sense in which we do have choice. I may live this tiny span of existence with God, or without him, and I shall discover sooner or later whether I have made the right choice—and it will be for all eternity.

## TRUST—WHATEVER!

*When my heart was grieved and my spirit embittered, I was senseless and ignorant; I was a brute beast before you. Yet I am always with you; you hold me by my right hand. You guide me with your counsel, and afterwards you will take me into glory. Whom have I in heaven but you? And earth has nothing I desire besides you. My flesh and my heart may fail, but God is the strength of my heart and my portion for ever.*
PSALM 73:21–26

If we can trust in God through difficulties, trouble and suffering, these can be truly instrumental in drawing us into a closer relationship with him, one which overrides all else. This passage shows that God's caring covers the whole span of our life—past, present and future. 'I am always with you,' says the writer to God.

Looking back on past troubles with this realisation, we see there is no room for bitterness or resentment. In retrospect, we can often see clearly that God was holding us up, though we may not have been aware of it at the time. All of us will at some time be perplexed, ill, lonely, weak or afraid. But we have a wise and loving God who will be with us in these troubles. And he will do wonderful things with our suffering if we ask him. We cannot escape suffering, but we have a wonderful Counsellor who will be our strength for ever.

In present troubles we can look back and look forward; either way we find reassurance and joy—now, in the midst of it all.


## THE BEST WINE—JOHN 2:1–11

*Nearby stood six stone water jars, the kind used by the Jews for ceremonial washing, each holding from twenty to thirty gallons. Jesus said to the servants, 'Fill the jars with water'; so they filled them to the brim.*

JOHN 2:6–7

In this well-known story, Jesus did not change water into ordinary wine at the Canaan wedding—he turned it into the best wine. No doubt, the host would have been grateful even for inferior wine. It was a typically gracious act of the Lord to save his host any embarrassment. But Jesus went beyond the simple need. He often does.

It is no surprise after this to find Jesus promising, 'I came that they may have life and have it to the full' (John 10:10). Here we are, caught up in our sins, unable to come into God's presence because of them, and Jesus, in his wonderful work at Calvary, not only sets us free, but 'is able to do immeasurably more than all we ask or imagine' (Ephesians 3:20). And not for this life only. In him we have a richer life now and also eternal life with him.

Not just wine—the best wine!

## A NEW CREATION—ISAIAH 65:17–25

*Behold, I will create new heavens and a new earth. The former things will not be remembered, nor will they come to mind.*

Isaiah 65:17

God did not cease all creative activity after the world was made. He continues to create in the present time.

We pray, 'Create and make in us new and contrite hearts' (see Psalm 51:10), and he does just that, remaking us when we are born again by the power of the Holy Spirit. In response to prayer, he creates love where there was hatred, hope where there was despair, confidence where there was fearfulness. He creates peace out of the storm of our conflicts, and joy alongside sorrow and suffering. He creates light out of the darkness we bring to him. Sometimes, mysteriously, he creates healthy bodily tissues out of diseased ones.

It is wonderful to go through each day expecting God to go on being creative—in world situations, in relationships, in our own lives. Something spoiled does not have to remain so for ever. As we read in Jeremiah, 'Cannot the potter remake the marred vessel he has made?' (see Jeremiah 18). Yes, he can.

## GOD'S PREROGATIVE—PSALM 35

*May those who delight in my vindication shout for joy and gladness; may they always say, 'The LORD be exalted, who delights in the well-being of his servant.'*
*My tongue will speak of your righteousness and of your praises all day long.*

Psalm 35:27–28

This is a difficult psalm, but it has something to say to all of us. David did feel hurt, angry and revengeful, as we may often do. But he himself does not try to get his own back. He does not attempt to bring down those who have wronged him. No, he brings his feelings to the Lord, recognising that vengeance belongs to him alone. We can do that.

David vows that he will give glory and praise and thanks to God when he is rescued from his enemies. We can do that, too. God alone is Judge. He is the judge of others and of ourselves. The best we can do is to bring our hurts and resentments to him, asking for grace to recognise our own faults, and seeking his healing of our wounded feelings. Do we do that?

## PSALM 91—ADAPTED AS A PERSONAL PRAYER

*He who dwells in the shelter of the Most High will rest in the shadow of the Almighty.*
*I will say of the LORD, 'He is my refuge and my fortress, my God, in whom I trust.'*
PSALM 91:1–2

Lord God, if I stay close to you I will rest in your shadow. You are my refuge, my fortress, my God and Heavenly Father. I trust you. You will cover me. Your faithfulness I will hold before me like a shield. I need not fear any terror by night or day. Being close to you, nothing can really harm me. Though I may suffer illness, accident or sorrow, it will be only as, in your eternal purpose, you allow. Nothing can separate me from you. Your angels will guard me and lift me up when trouble comes. With you I can overcome evil and disaster. Because I love you, and acknowledge your name, you will rescue me and protect me. When I call on you, you will answer me. Eternal life will be mine, and the joy of your presence for ever, for by grace I have been saved through faith in Jesus Christ, my Saviour. Thank you, O my God.


## FRIENDS OF GOD

*I have called you friends.*
JOHN 15:15

Jesus speaks these words to his disciples as the time draws near for him to leave them and face death. In this beautiful chapter of John's Gospel, it is just one of the treasures from the lips of Jesus. To be a friend of Jesus is, of course, to be a friend of God. What does it mean to be a friend?

We do not betray a friend.

We fight to defend the name of a friend.

We delight to talk to, and talk about, a friend.

We want to help a friend, and to share what we have.

We want to be in the company of a friend.

We take delight in giving to a friend.

There is a wonderful bond of love and trust between friends. All this and more. And Jesus is our friend!

In our relationship with God, it follows that we shall be loyal, prayerful, willing to serve and to witness, longing to understand him more and more, and to be increasingly aware of him; we shall grow in love, and live in joy and trust; we shall cheerfully give to him our time, talents and money; we shall worship God, too, as only he should be worshipped.

Jesus, our friend, has promised never to leave or forsake us. Can we make that promise to him?

## PONDERING

*[Joseph's] brothers were jealous of him, but his father kept the matter in mind.*

GENESIS 37:11

*Mary treasured up all these things and pondered them in her heart.*

LUKE 2:19

A believer in God, and in tune with him, will be much more likely to perceive the deep significance of events and circumstances than an unbeliever, who may dismiss them as mere coincidences. A Christian will often observe the hand of God working out his purposes. We need to cultivate this sensitivity so that we may respond in line with his will. It may concern something in our own lives, or a matter about which we need to pray on behalf of someone else.

It is valuable to make a regular study of the Bible, prayerfully, meditatively and expectantly. Intellectual understanding is not enough if we are to find its relevance to our own lives. We need to 'ponder it in our hearts'.

This is a deeply enriching experience.

## A MEDITATION ON PSALM 23

*The LORD is my shepherd, I shall not be in want. He makes me lie down in green pastures, he leads me beside quiet waters, he restores my soul. He guides me in paths of righteousness for his name's sake.*

PSALM 23:1–3

My Lord and Shepherd makes me lie down in green pastures—resting, peaceful, calm, secure. Why? Because he knows my need and is always on watch, alert, aware. I can have a place of green pastures always with me, deep within myself. I can lie down there in safety and quiet whatever I am doing and wherever I am. Yes, there will be valleys of darkness, and death of the body is a certainty; but my shepherd will always be there, so I need not fear. I shall always be safe with his rod and staff to discipline, guard and rescue me. I can even have a meal in peace and safety in the midst of danger! He is on watch and in control while my physical needs are met. His wonderful goodness and love, which has been with me from the moment I was born, will continue to follow me till the end of my days. Guided in doing his will, I will always be in his presence and, finally, come home to him and stay there for ever.

So may I rest in the Lord always.

## JESUS IS IN THE BOAT—LUKE 8:22–25

*As they sailed, [Jesus] fell asleep. A squall came down on the lake, so that the boat was being swamped, and they were in great danger.*

LUKE 8:23

The disciples were obeying their Master in setting out to cross the lake, but this did not mean immunity from the typical storms, and they found themselves in the middle of one. Jesus was sleeping, unconcerned. But the men were terrified. 'Where is your faith?' Jesus asked when they had woken him. Nevertheless, he did calm the storm. He cared about their weakness and fear.

The fact that Jesus is in my boat does not make me immune from the storms of life. But it does mean that I need never fear them. Yes, it may get rough, but he will not let me be overwhelmed as long as I call upon him.

## MARTHA AND MARY—LUKE 10:38–42

*But Martha was distracted by all the preparations that had to be made. She came to him and asked, 'Lord, don't you care that my sister has left me to do the work by myself? Tell her to help me!'*
LUKE 10:40

Sometimes we debate the relative merits of these two sisters. Often we think that Martha was regarded unfairly by Jesus, and we feel sorry for her.

The teaching of Jesus here is certainly that our relationship with himself is the most important thing. What we are is more important than what we do. Too much pride can be invested in the doing—though, of course, our faith will lead to 'good works' as is made so clear in Ephesians 2:10: 'For we are God's workmanship, created in Christ Jesus to do good works, which God prepared in advance for us to do.' If we spend time with Jesus, we shall discern what it is he wants us to do, and we shall do it in confidence and in humility and peace.

Surely, we need to identify with both sisters, sometimes just being with Jesus, and at other times busy serving him.

## PRAYING WITH PSALM 31:1–5

*In you, O LORD, I have taken refuge; let me never be put to shame; deliver me in your righteousness.*

PSALM 31:1

David asks nine specific things of God: deliverance, a listening ear; rescue; hiding; defence; leading; guidance; freeing; redeeming. As believers, we know that we start from the position of being loved and accepted by God, and that he listens to us. So we can pray according to David's pattern here:

Heavenly Father, deliver us from all that would harm our relationship with you. Rescue us from evil, within and without; hide us in your shelter when we are afraid; keep us safe in your fortress, and defend us in your power and love. Free us from all that hinders us from living fully for you; lead us out in trust and in your protection, and guide us in all things. Give us confidence to live joyfully in the knowledge of your faithfulness and care. Thank you that our times are in your hands. Help us to remember you in good times and bad, for the glory of your name.

## BE STILL

*Be still and know that I am God. I will be exalted in the earth.*

PSALM 46:10

God will be exalted among nations and on earth. Nothing can thwart his ultimate purposes. Therefore we can really be still and have inward peace, knowing that he is God, the omnipotent Creator and Redeemer, no matter how great the chaos reigning on earth might be.

God's Word assures us that this is true for each of us today. We may experience conflict, discord, suffering; but none of this can prevail against his purposes for the good of those who own his lordship.


## HARMONY

*Live in harmony with one another.*

1 PETER 3:8

Think of an orchestra. No matter how beautiful the melody played by each instrument, if each were to play without reference to the others, what horrible discord would result! To achieve harmony, all eyes must be on the one conductor.

The church is all about harmony—harmony in relationships, each member aware of and working with the others. And, as in an orchestra, our eyes need to be always on our Divine Conductor.

This is a far cry from the idea that some people have of 'keeping themselves to themselves', going their own way. This is like every member of the orchestra playing a different tune, all at the same time!

In the church, we are intimately related to one another and to Christ himself—concerned for one another.

Sadly, there is often discord within the church family, just as sometimes there is in human families. The example of Euodia and Syntyche in Philippians 4:2 is a sad testimony to this. We need to work hard at harmonising with one another and to have the love of God bind us together in a fellowship which is so attractive that 'outsiders' are drawn in to discover the secret of such harmony.

## MUTUAL COMFORT

*Praise be to the God and Father of our Lord Jesus Christ, the Father of compassion and the God of all comfort, who comforts us in all our troubles so that we can comfort those in any trouble with the comfort we ourselves have received from God.*

2 CORINTHIANS 1:3–4

We are bound to suffer with others if we have any compassion at all. As Christians, our compassion will go deeper, for we know the compassion of Christ for us. Because of this, we shall be able to offer greater comfort to those who suffer.

Christ loves us, and he gives us love for others. This is a lovely picture of 'give and take' between God, ourselves and others.

## GOD'S WONDERFUL DEEDS SEEN IN PSALM 81

*Sing for joy to God our strength; shout aloud to the God of Jacob!*

PSALM 81:1

He is our strength (verse 1);

He removes burdens (verse 6);

He rescues and answers when we call (verse 7);

He tests us (verse 7);

He speaks to warn us (verse 8), to lead us (verse 13), to subdue the enemy (verse 14);

He feeds and satisfies us (verse 16);

This is the LORD, OUR GOD (verse 10)! He will have all things for our good. We have every reason to sing for joy, as the psalmist encourages us to do.


## FEAR

*... God has said, 'Never will I leave you; never will I forsake you.'*
*So we say with confidence, 'The Lord is my helper; I will not be*
*afraid. What can man do to me?'*

HEBREWS 13:5–6


We are all prone to fear at one time or another, sometimes quite irrationally. Fear is very prominent in the pages of the Bible, and very much accepted as a human condition. We read, '*when* I am afraid'—not '*if* I am afraid'. Of course, there is a type of fear that is essential for our preservation, or perfectly reasonable in dangerous circumstances; but some fear is destructive.

The whole Passion Story is threaded through with fear of some kind, and we see it often in the Gospel accounts: The disciples deserted Jesus because they were scared; Peter denied Jesus because he was frightened for himself; Pilate was afraid of his superiors and acted against his own conscience; Judas Iscariot was afraid of his own condemning conscience and committed suicide.

Then there was the man called Joseph, who was a secret disciple because he was a member of the Sanhedrin and he feared for his reputation. Nicodemus believed in Jesus, but was afraid to follow him openly. Who has not known fears such as these and others? What is the antidote? We will find it in trusting Jesus and his promises.


## SEA SHELLS

*He has made everything beautiful in its time. He has also set eternity in the hearts of men; yet they cannot fathom what God has done from beginning to end.*

ECCLESIASTES 3:11

I have a particularly beautiful shell, delicately coloured in pale shades of pink and creamy-brown, intricately curved into a wondrous shape. When I hold it in my hand, I feel I catch a glimpse of our wonderful Creator. Could any human hand or modern machinery emulate it, I wonder? But it was made by a simple sea slug!

To contemplate this little fragment of our complex world is to marvel at the mystery of the Creator God. He is awesomely beyond our imagination and comprehension. Since he has taken such care in giving a simple creature the skill to make its beautiful 'house', can we doubt his absolute love and concern for us? We have been given the uniquely human gift of wonder, and we direct it first to the Creator, and then to all his works.

In the words of Psalm 8:1, we may indeed say: 'O LORD, our Lord, how majestic is your name in all the earth!'

## MARTYRDOM FOR CHRIST—ACTS 14:19–22

*They stoned Paul and dragged him outside the city, thinking he was dead.*

ACTS 14:19

Paul's physical suffering is almost unimaginable—the lacerations and bruising and his final collapse. His tormentors, believing him to be dead, dragged his sore, bleeding body along the ground to get him outside the city.

Did his friends kneel and pray around him, I wonder? And did the Lord heal him? He must have done, I think, because the terribly damaged man got up and went back into the city! And the next day he travelled on to continue preaching.

This was not the only suffering that this man of God endured, as we know from other accounts. How great his faith and love for the Lord to drive him on under such circumstances!

## GOD'S TEMPLE—2 SAMUEL 7:1–12

*That night the word of the LORD came to Nathan, saying: 'Go and tell my servant David, "This is what the LORD says: Are you the one to build me a house to dwell in?"'*

2 SAMUEL 7:4–5

The only home God condescends to need is in our hearts. He says, in this passage, 'I have been with you wherever you have gone.' The great temple was to be built by another, and David has to accept that, just as we often have to accept a lesser role in God's work. Even when the temple was built, Solomon has doubts about God's need of it, saying, 'But will God really dwell on earth? The heavens, even the highest heaven, cannot contain you. How much less this temple that I have built' (1 Kings 8:27). The apostle Paul, writing to the Corinthians, says, 'We are the temple of the living God.' We—you and I!

We so often get it wrong. We think God needs all that we need, but he himself is the giver of all things. What he asks of us is to make room in our hearts for him. 'My son, give me your heart and let your eyes keep to my ways' (Proverbs 23:26).

## A SUMMARY OF LOVE—1 JOHN 4:7–21

*Dear friends, let us love one another, for love comes from God. Everyone who loves has been born of God and knows God.*

1 JOHN 4:7

Love comes from God, who himself is love. Only those who love have been born of God and know him. God demonstrated his love by sending Jesus to be our Saviour and to bring us to eternal life. God first loved us, not we him. Because of his love, we can and must love one another. If we acknowledge Jesus as the Son of God and love one another, God lives in us and we live in him. God's love finds significant expression in and through our lives. If we truly love, we need not fear judgement. Love for our fellow Christians is proof of our love for God.

## SPIRITUAL HARVEST—HEBREWS 12:7–11

*Endure hardship as discipline; God is treating you as sons. For what son is not disciplined by his father?*

HEBREWS 12:7

How does God discipline us? Perhaps by humbling us by our not receiving the recognition we feel we deserve; allowing us to be scorned for our faith; showing us our weakness; allowing us to fail when we attempt a task before prayer for guidance; allowing things to happen to our bodies that we do not understand, and so on—God has no need to manufacture circumstances, for we make enough mistakes to provide material for his discipline!

No doubt we agree with the writer to the Hebrews that 'no discipline seems pleasant at the time, but painful.' We find it difficult even when we recognise that God is treating us as his children. But look at the harvest to be gained if we learn from it: 'Later on, however, it produces a harvest of righteousness and peace for those who have been trained by it.' (verse 11).

## FAIR PLAY—MATTHEW 18:21–35

*'You wicked servant ... I cancelled all that debt of yours because you begged me to. Shouldn't you have had mercy on your fellow-servant just as I had on you?'*

MATTHEW 18:32

God has forgiven us so much. How can we refuse forgiveness to others whose faults are so small in comparison? This parable teaches us that God is angry at our failure to forgive, and we put ourselves in danger of forfeiting his forgiveness of us.

Once again we are faced with the command to be merciful out of love. How can we not love one another in the face of God's great love for us? If we fail to forgive, that sin may well be greater than that of the one who wrongs us.

An important point in the story is that the king does not forgive until the debtor shows repentance, seeks the king's mercy and vows to put matters right.


## THE WAY

*You know the way to the place where I am going.*

John 14:4


Jesus said this to his disciples shortly before his death on the cross. But they did not know, did not understand, in spite of all the time they had spent with him.

Here we have the advantage, for we have the Bible, the Word of God, and can read it and meditate upon it in depth. The Holy Spirit speaks to us through it, and we know the way. All we have to do is turn from our sins, believe in Jesus, and we shall, after this life, be with him for ever (John 3:16). It is that simple!


## LOST FOR WORDS

*We do not know what we ought to pray, but the Spirit himself intercedes for us.*

Romans 8:26


We sometimes pray foolishly, blindly, selfishly, and we may indeed be thankful when God does not answer such prayers. To bring to the Father our deepest needs with the desire that his perfect will be done is, we may be sure, pleasing to him.

Sometimes we are lost for words. We do not know how to pray. Then the Holy Spirit comes to our aid. He is one with God, one with Jesus Christ, and he discerns our innermost thoughts and longings and brings them to the Father.

There is mystery here, and comfort, too. We may not fully comprehend; but the fact that we do not understand the workings of television, computers, washing machines and other such wonders of our age, does not stop us from using them!

So let us give thanks for God's amazing blessings—material, yes, but above all spiritual blessings.

## FROM CHRYSALIS TO BUTTERFLY

*Do not conform any longer to the pattern of this world, but be transformed by the renewing of your mind. Then you will be able to test and approve what God's will is—his good, pleasing and perfect will.*

ROMANS 12:2

'Be transformed,' says the apostle Paul. Leave the chrysalis and become a butterfly—free!

We need not go on with the same old habits and limitations for ever. God's will for us—now—is that we should be holy and pleasing to him. We cannot achieve this in our own strength any more than a pupa can will its own transformation. But once we have discovered what God's will is for us, we can work with him to do the work of changing us.

God's will may not always seem to us good, pleasing and perfect; there is pain and suffering and stress. But a continuous transformation will be taking place in his power. We do not always recognise the changes in our own nature, nor do we see them happening within the butterfly pupa. Yet, as we offer ourselves to God, he will renew our minds and transform our lives. We shall fly!


## THE PERFECT PEACE OF CHRIST

*Peace I leave with you; my peace I give you. I do not give to you as the world gives. Do not let your hearts be troubled and do not be afraid.*

JOHN 14:27

What was that quality of peace which Jesus possessed and which he promised to us, his followers? One source, surely, was his way of living each moment to the full, working with—or simply enjoying—the present circumstances, not 'crossing bridges before he came to them'.

There is peace for us in accepting the present moment and living that to the full for the glory of God. And this is true even in times of simply enduring.

Another source of Jesus' peace was surely the assurance that all things were ultimately in the Father's hands, and that his victory— and ours—is certain whatever the trials that beset him and us.

For Jesus, he knew that rejection and a cruel death lay ahead; yet he had peace. Yes, he suffered the agony of Gethsemane, for he was fully human. But we read in Hebrews 12:2, 'for the joy that was set before him' he endured the cross.

Amazing, that word 'joy'! But he knew that the Father's will was being accomplished for all his people through his own obedience. Our joy and peace, too, come from knowing that, whatever trials we experience now, God's will is being accomplished in us as we closely follow Jesus.

## THE CHOSEN WAY

*All the ways of the Lord are loving and faithful for those who*
*keep his covenant ... Who, then, is the [one] who fears the* LORD?
*He will instruct him in the way chosen for him.*

PSALM 25:10, 12

In verse 11, David asks God to forgive his sin, which, he says, is great. He knows he has digressed from God's way.

The really important thing in life is that we should go in the way chosen for us by God. But how will we know? The Lord will instruct us. In Psalm 119:105, the writer says God gives us a lamp to light up the path; in Isaiah 30:21, we read that we have ears attuned to God's voice saying, 'This is the way'; Jeremiah 10:23 tells us that our life is not our own, and 'it is not for us to direct our steps'—how could we, with our limited vision?

The emphasis in all this is God's Word. It has been given to us, passed down through the ages in written form—the Bible—and those with a right fear of God will read that Word avidly for instruction and guidance. We have the Holy Spirit, too, who lives in us and speaks in the Bible to hearts that are open. We are certainly not left without help with our 'route' if we desire it.

We may not know it at the time, but the path chosen for us will undoubtedly be the best one—always.

## FAITH AND HOPE

*Faith is being sure of what we hope for and certain of what we do not see.*

HEBREWS 11:1

Is there anything on earth that we hope for, knowing that we shall receive it, or that it will come to pass? We may hope for health, security, wealth, success, the wellbeing of loved ones and all other benefits. But we are by no means certain that our hopes will be fulfilled. Often we are dogged by underlying fear and uncertainty. Who has not experienced this?

Christian hope is a different matter. The outcome—salvation in Christ—is promised, sure. It is an expectant hope of something assured, and that hope is a source of joy and strength. God is faithful and will fulfil all his promises, and there are many of these in the Scriptures.

We say of earthly things, 'Seeing is believing.' But for the Christian it is the other way round. Because of our faith, we believe in those things as yet unseen. To walk in faith and trust is to know certainty, and in that certainty we find peace.


## FROM SERVANT TO FRIEND

*I no longer call you servants ... Instead, I have called you friends.*

JOHN 15:15

Jesus is speaking here to his disciples, but no less to us today. We are called to follow his example of service, as he made clear at the foot washing during the Last Supper.

To be Christ's friend does not exclude readiness to be his slave—

yes, slave. A slave is bound to the master, with no rights and no pay except what is freely given. Our Master rewards us bountifully, and is truly a friend above all friends.

Can we grasp the wonder of this—friends of Jesus, the Son of God? Could we really want freedom from him, whatever the cost?

## A VISUAL AID!—ACTS 3:6–8

*Peter said to the crippled beggar, 'Silver or gold I do not have, but what I have I give you. In the name of Jesus Christ of Nazareth, walk.' And he did.*

ACTS 3:6

In Acts 3 and 4, Peter and John have a 'visual aid'—a crippled man—and this becomes the starting point for two sermons, first to the onlookers, and then to the authorities.

We can use this act of healing as an illustration of God's work in our salvation: All of us are 'crippled' from birth by sin, helpless to save ourselves. Like the beggar in this account, we have to be 'carried'—brought to God through Christ by the action of the Holy Spirit. It may be through someone else that we meet Christ, but it is still the Spirit at work.

The man in the story expected the wrong thing—money for his material needs. But God knew his deeper need, and he knows ours. We cannot expect freedom from life's troubles and burdens; they will always be with us. If that is what we want when we come to Christ, we are in for a big disappointment.

When God meets our needs as he sees them, then we shall be truly whole. The result will be like that of this cripple— spontaneous praise of God—and it will be contagious! All will recognise that it is a work of God. We shall not be able to hold back in our witness to that fact, and, just as the beggar's praise of God led to a sermon resulting in mass conversions, so we may cause many others to believe in him.

## KNOWN BY NAME

*He calls his own sheep by name and leads them out. When he has brought out all his own, he goes on ahead of them, and the sheep follow him because they know his voice.*

JOHN 10:3–4

Jesus is speaking of himself as the true shepherd. It is a lovely picture of familiarity with his own sheep. He knows each of them by name, and he knows your name and mine!

It is a picture of activity, too—not of staying within the sheep pen, protected and safe, but of going out into life, obedient to the call of the shepherd and following where he goes.

Listening to his voice, hearing his Word, the Bible, all will be well wherever we go, for he himself is leading us. Knowing his care for us, we can go willingly and trustingly.

## REAL JOY—JOHN 15:9–17

*I have told you this so that my joy may be in you and that your joy may be complete.*

JOHN 15:11

Jesus has been telling his disciples that he has loved them just as the Father has loved him. If they obey him, they will remain in his love.

This joy that Jesus gives has little to do with laughter, but everything to do with peace and contentment in all circumstances. There is a wonderful example of this in Habakkuk 3:17–19: The prophet is foreseeing the devastating time when the crops and the livestock fail, yet he says, 'I will rejoice in the LORD.' He is not, of course, rejoicing because of the disaster, but in spite of it. He rejoices in the sheer wonder of God as his saviour and his strength.

We, too, can rejoice even in the midst of problems, pains and grief because we have Jesus Christ as our Saviour, and our Friend.

## NO FEAR

*Jesus said, 'In this world you will have trouble. But take heart! I have overcome the world.'*

JOHN 16:33

Though we hear of wars, conflicts and atrocities in the world, we are not to be alarmed, for God is the refuge and strength of all who trust in him, for he is present in every trouble. We can shelter under the cover of his wings through all the storms of life— thunder and lightning, or personal and international storms. The life of every believer is in the Lord's hands. We need not fear bad news or any disaster. Our hearts can be steadfast, trusting in him. We can know peace even in the midst of trouble.

All this seems too good to be true, doesn't it? But no—Jesus has finally overcome the world and, hard though it sometimes is, we can hope in him in everything.

There is similar encouragement in 2 Chronicles 16:9: 'For the eyes of the LORD range throughout the earth to strengthen those whose hearts are fully committed to him.' He sees. He knows.

God-fearing people will always place every problem in his hands, for the battle against evil is always in his power, and his alone. Our job is to pray when disaster strikes and, in faith, to praise God even before the victory is ours. Thus prepared, we need no longer fear. And when the disaster is past, and people see how God has been at work in it, all the glory will be his. What is more, our faith will be stronger than ever.

## THE ALL-SEEING GOD

*The eyes of the LORD are everywhere.*
PROVERBS 15:3

You are the God who sees me. (Genesis 16:13)
You have searched me and you know me. (Psalm 139:1)
God knows your hearts. (Luke 16:15)
[Jesus] knew all men. (John 2:24)
Are we happy for God to know us completely—the good and the bad? Some people are uncomfortable with this, even those perhaps not guilty of any major sin. But God-fearing people can welcome this transparency before God, for we know that he understands our human condition, and that he forgives us every time we repent of any sin. What is more, it is to protect and strengthen us that the Lord keeps an eye on us. He does, after all, love us!

## HOLY JOY

*Serve the Lord with fear and rejoice with trembling.*
PSALM 2:11

Holy joy is tempered with healthy fear. Humanly speaking, joy in a relationship is tinged with an innate, interior fear of its ending, but it is not so with God. He will never change, and the relationship is for all eternity.

This relationship with God has at its heart a realisation of his holiness, and, in contrast, our own sinfulness, leading to reverent fear. We rejoice because we are accepted by God in spite of our tendency to go our own way. God is not blind to our sin. In Deuteronomy 4:24 we read that he is a consuming fire. But he is at work in our lives and will reshape and sanctify us. Why? Because he made us and loves us, and intends that we should worship him in reverence and awe.

Our love for God provides no immunity from his just and righteous anger. It is appropriate that we rejoice—but with trembling.

## PRAYER—BASED ON 2 CORINTHIANS 10:3–5

*For though we live in the world, we do not wage war as the world does. The weapons we fight with are not the weapons of the world. On the contrary, they have divine power to demolish strongholds. We demolish arguments and every pretension that sets itself up against the knowledge of God, and we take captive every thought to make it obedient to Christ.*

2 CORINTHIANS 10:3–5

Lord, help us in our ministry for you to show the meekness and gentleness that was your hallmark. But let us be bold to take up the sword of the Spirit and use it to pierce to the heart of every matter; to cut away the rank growth of worldliness that inhibits the free working of your Spirit; to expose your truth. May we wield it fearlessly to wage war against all the powers of darkness. And let us not fear to use it on ourselves, Lord. Take every thought captive, and help us to obey your commands, for the honour and glory of your holy name. Amen.


## A RELUCTANT PREACHER

*Forty more days and Nineveh will be destroyed.*
JONAH 3:4

Such a short sermon! But they were God's words proclaimed in his power, and the response was dramatic.

How awesome for Jonah to be the one chosen to speak the words that saved so many souls! Yet he did not feel this. He had been disobedient to God's command in the first place, and had run away. Now he felt let down—if God was going to save all these people anyway, why was he sent back to Nineveh?

But all through the pages of Scripture we see that God uses people—maybe you and me—to proclaim his message. The people of Nineveh were changed through Jonah's God-given words. They escaped punishment. God intended that they should repent, and Jonah was the chosen channel.

How glad we should be for the privilege of being such instruments in his hand!

## SPIRITUAL ATHLETICS—THOUGHTS FROM
## 1 CORINTHIANS 9 AND HEBREWS 12

*In a race all runners run, but only one gets the prize.*

1 CORINTHIANS 9:24–25

*Let us throw off everything that hinders ... and run with
perseverance the race marked out for us. Let us fix our eyes on
Jesus.*

HEBREWS 12:1–2

In any athletic event, only one gets the first prize, yes. But in the 'race' of our spiritual journey, all runners receive a prize at the finishing line—'the crown that will last for ever'.

Modern athletes strip down to the barest necessities, streamlined for maximum progress. We, too, in life's race, need to see that we are not encumbered by worldly cares and possessions. And, of course, it is important to make sure we are on the right track—'the race marked out for us'. We shall not win if we run on a different route. Nor are we likely to win if we continually look back to see how the others are doing. We need to 'fix our eyes on Jesus' all the time.

Elsewhere, the apostle Paul uses a different metaphor—that of a goal. It is possible to run magnificently with the ball, evading all opposition, and score a goal for the other side because we have run in the wrong direction! If we keep our eyes on Jesus, we shall be sure of going in the intended direction—heavenwards.

Perseverance is important, too. This entails strict training and some self-denial. For the Christian 'race', Bible reading, prayer and public worship will be the mainstay of this. But, in addition, we shall find that this life provides all the material we need to practise discipline and trust, and to increase our strength. Every problem, every trouble, is an opportunity for spiritual progress if we look to the Lord to use it.


## ROUGH STONES

*In building the temple, only blocks dressed at the quarry were used, and no hammer, chisel or any other iron tool was heard at the temple site while it was being built.*

1 KINGS 6:7


The work on the rough stone takes place away from the temple site, probably out of a sense of reverence.

This is only partly the case where the Christian church is concerned. We are the stones that make up the church. The apostle Peter called us 'living stones' being built into a spiritual house to be a holy priesthood, offering spiritual sacrifices acceptable to God through Jesus Christ (1 Peter 2:5). Some of the work on rough stones takes place away from the building itself, but a good deal of this work takes place within it, too.

God is at work day by day, wherever we are, shaping us. This is important if we are to 'fit together' when we meet for Sunday worship. Our rough edges need to be smoothed. More work is done within the church fellowship as we hear the word of God, sing his praises and pray together. This work is never finished in this life.

In a deeper sense, the work on the building of the church concerns the final outcome—the eternal city, for which we are being prepared. We read in Revelation 21 that the City of God is composed of many kinds of stone, each precious, each prepared by God. Each piece of rough and craggy stone has to be cut to size and polished. There are many layers in this 'building', and it does not matter in which layer we are placed; each forms a foundation for others and is essential to the whole.

God has prepared me; he knows where I am and how I fit—but only, of course, works on me in the quarry of my everyday life and worship.

## OUR REFUGE—PSALM 46:1–3

*God is our refuge and strength … Therefore we will not fear though the earth give way and the mountains fall into the heart of the sea.*
PSALM 46:1–2

How contemporary this psalm is! In this violent nuclear age, it does not seem at all impossible that the earth will give way and the mountains crumble. Yet the writer is full of hope—his confidence is in God.

The desolations of which he speaks can be personal as well as national and worldwide. Perhaps God means to use them to bring us to our senses, to get our priorities right. He is in control of the world's ultimate destiny—and our own—and he is an ever-present help in trouble.

There may be little we can do about the world situation in practical terms, and not much we can do to control our own circumstances. But we can certainly pray to the God of all power and grace.

## PRAISE IN OLD AGE

*When I said, 'My foot is slipping', your love, O LORD, supported me. When anxiety was great within me, your consolation brought joy to my soul.*

PSALM 94:18–19

One of the benefits of ageing is that there are more and more times when we can look back and see how God has wonderfully been at work in our lives, guiding and supporting us. What a boost to our faith this is, and what cause for thankfulness!

Jesus says, 'He who has been forgiven little loves little' (Luke 7:47). How our love grows with age as we remember how very much in our lives has needed to be forgiven! So it will be for all our days. If we can hold in our hearts that joy, that love and gratitude to God, we shall avoid the bitterness that can creep in as a result of the trials of old age.

## OVERFLOWING HOPE

*Overflow with hope by the power of the Holy Spirit.*

ROMANS 15:13

In this passage, the apostle Paul refers to the God of hope. He it is who will fill us to overflowing. An overflowing vessel has no room for anything to dilute and spoil it, and nothing can be added. If we overflow with hope, there will be no room for doubt, depression, anxiety or despair. What is more, that hope will spill over into other people's lives. (Can you carry a cup filled to the top without spilling any?)

Since filling is the work of the Holy Spirit, we need to offer ourselves fully to him by a conscious act of will. Then we shall be full of hope—in this life, and for the next, for all eternity. And this hope is not a vague longing for something we might or might not have. No, it is a sure and certain hope, based on God's promises, and in which we can rejoice—now!

## DOES GOD CARE?

*Teacher, don't you care …?*
MARK 4:38

*Cast all your anxiety on him because he cares for you.*
1 PETER 5:7

This has been the cry of people through the ages—the Israelites on their long desert journey to the Promised Land; the disciples on the stormy lake; Martha and Mary, when Jesus took so long to come to their brother, Lazarus, so that he died. We ask it when we are anxious and fearful, and our prayers seem to go unanswered.

Of course the Lord cares, as we know from many accounts in the Bible. But the things that bother us are not always serious in his eyes. God's thoughts and ways are higher than ours. We get our priorities wrong, and maybe we do not trust enough, so we do not wait for him to act.

When God holds back his help, perhaps he is teaching us that we need not have got into a certain situation, or that he intends to use it in a way we had not envisaged.

O, that we might learn to wait upon his timing—quietly resting in the assurance of his presence, whatever the circumstances. He knows. He cares.

## CONTENT WITH MY LOT?

*LORD, you have assigned me my portion and my cup.*
PSALM 16:5

A re we happy with our circumstances? Is God really behind every experience, the good and the bad? As far as we know, is all within his purpose for us?

If we believe this, it can transform our whole response to life. In sickness, sorrow or trouble of any kind, we will put our trust in him, waiting patiently and hopefully for whatever good he intends to bring out of it. In joyful, secure times, we will be filled with thankfulness and praise. And when we endure any hardship in his ever-present strength, we shall grow in spiritual stature.

In Psalm 73:25, the writer says, 'Whom have I in heaven but you, and earth has nothing I desire besides you. My flesh and my heart may fail, but God is the strength of my heart and my portion for ever.' Can we affirm this?

In Psalm 23, David confidently says, 'Even though I walk through the valley of the shadow of death, I will fear no evil, for you are with me.' Do we believe this?

God's promise to Jeremiah (see chapter 29:11) is for us, too: ' I know the plans I have for you … plans to prosper you and not to harm you, plans to give you hope and a future.'

Yes, we can trust the One who has 'assigned us our portion and our cup'—he is in control of our lives. We need not be anxious— whatever the outcome may be.

## PERSECUTION A BLESSING?

*Blessed are you when people ... persecute you because of me.*
*Rejoice and be glad.*

MATTHEW 5:11–12

Can we imagine encouraging our best friends to walk right into trouble, persecution and probable death? That is what Jesus did. He loved his disciples, and yet he expected them to take the path of deliberate suffering and difficulty. Why? Because he knew that the reward would far exceed the sufferings of the present time.

He taught them that to love their own life would mean losing it, whereas hating their life in this world would mean keeping it for eternity (John 12:25). This means that love of God must come before everything else. Always, Christ has our deepest welfare at heart. He does not have our limited vision and values. No suffering is wasted, especially if it is for Christ. For him, it was not an end, but the route to a glorious purpose to be achieved for the benefit of all.


## CHRIST OUR 'SPONSOR'

*Nothing impure will ever enter [the kingdom of God].*

REVELATION 21:27

*Created to be like God in true righteousness and holiness.*

EPHESIANS 4:24

It is a sad fact that we, who were meant to live in direct fellowship with God—holy, obedient, blameless—are, through innate sin, not fit in ourselves to come near to God. We can come into his presence only, so to speak, on the 'sponsorship' of Christ.

We are not acceptable to God in our own right, but only as

friends and followers of Christ. He has paid the price—our 'entrance fee'—into the kingdom. In the application of redemption, he has given us his own righteousness and holiness.

Thank God for Jesus—and for the remarkable truth of justification by faith!

## OUR SPIRITUAL CLOTHES

*Do not worry about ... what you will wear.*

MATTHEW 6:25

Jesus is teaching the disciples to think about what really matters in life, and what we wear is not one of them—at least, not in a literal sense. But clothes—spiritual clothes—are amazingly important in the Scriptures. The clothes that really matter are those given by God. Consider these:

The Lord sent Isaiah to give his people, among other things, 'a garment of praise instead of despair.' Isaiah says of himself, too, 'My soul rejoices in God, for he has clothed me with garments of salvation and arrayed me in a robe of righteousness' (Isaiah 61:3,10). We are encouraged to 'clothe ourselves with splendour' (Psalm 45:3); 'with compassion' (Colossians 3:12); 'with humility' (1 Peter 5:5); 'with the Lord Jesus' (Romans 13:14).

Before his ascension into heaven after his resurrection, Jesus told his disciples to stay in the city before starting their work of witness until they had been 'clothed with power from on high' (Luke 24:49).

Job, looking back on his life before all his suffering began, said, 'I put on righteousness as my clothing; justice was my robe and my turban' (Job 29:14).

God has a rich and wonderful wardrobe: praise, salvation, righteousness, splendour, strength, compassion, humility, power and justice, the Lord Jesus!

But beware! Satan, too, provides clothes—garments of disguise. Jesus warns that false prophets, who will lead his people astray, 'come to you in sheep's clothing, but inwardly they are ferocious wolves' (Matthew 7:15).

We need to be very discerning where such spiritual clothes are concerned.

## LASTING VALUES

*The world and its desires pass away, but the [one] who does the will of God lives for ever.*

1 JOHN 2:17

The day I accepted Jesus as Lord, I embarked upon the journey of eternal life. I am living on that plane now—today and every day—freed from the constraints and limitations of a purely earthly existence, in the deepest sense.

My mind and spirit can roam free whatever my bodily condition, for the body is, for the time being, temporary. But I need constant reminders that this means a different perspective on all my thinking and doing and intentions. It means a radical pruning of all that is superfluous; it means living simply. This does not mean cutting out all enjoyment, but avoiding excesses and extravagance for myself. It means avoiding anxiety about my age, my health, my future; all these are temporary. Taking due thought and care, certainly, but only as God guides.

To live like this is to accept the unchangeable, and to rejoice in everything good in God's sight. Therein lies true peace, joy and contentment.


## THE VERY BEST—PHILIPPIANS 3:7–11

*I consider everything a loss compared to the surpassing greatness of knowing Christ Jesus my Lord, for whose sake I have lost all things. I consider them rubbish, that I may gain Christ and be found in him. I want to know Christ ... and the fellowship of sharing in his sufferings.*

PHILIPPIANS 3:8–10

In this great passage, Paul is using the strongest possible words of comparison: knowing Christ is not only better than any worldly gain; it is the only thing that really matters. By comparison, everything else, he says, is to him rubbish! What he previously valued is not just less good, but total loss (verse 8).

How many of us can claim to value the knowledge of Christ that much, I wonder. Even though knowing Christ means sharing in his sufferings, Paul still has a deep desire to know him (verse 10).

This is not knowledge about Christ, but knowing him personally, intimately and with commitment, such as we might humanly feel towards a dearly loved friend. Paul yearns for the 'fellowship of sharing in' Christ's sufferings. To suffer with Christ brings us as close as we could possibly be to our Lord.

Paul wants, too, to be 'found in him'—being in continual union with him. So many things—and people—compete for our attention and value and love in this life. I am sure that God means us to enjoy what is good, but if these take priority over our love for Christ, then we are missing out on the very best: a relationship with the Lord.

This may remind us of the man who found a pearl of great price and went and sold everything he had in order to possess that pearl (Matthew 13:46).

Would we—do we—value Christ that much?

## SUCH A SMALL ARMY!—JUDGES 7

*The LORD said to Gideon, 'You have too many men for me to deliver Midian into their hands. In order that Israel may not boast against me that her own strength has saved her, announce now to the people, "Anyone who trembles with fear may turn back and leave Mount Gilead."' So twenty-two thousand men left, while ten thousand remained.*

JUDGES 7:2–3

The Midianites had invaded and oppressed the Israelites and had to be repelled. Gideon was God's man to lead the fight.

Israel had a great army; but God set up a plan to select only three hundred men 'in order that Israel may not boast … that her own strength had saved her.' It seemed an impossibly small army but, just as the Lord had promised, it was enough. The Midianites were overcome.

The Lord's strength is not in numbers. As God said to the apostle Paul, many years later, 'My power is made perfect in weakness.' (2 Corinthians 12:9).

If God used only the strong and influential for his work, they would be able to boast in themselves, giving none of the glory to God. Paul confessed that he was no great speaker in himself; he spoke in the power of God. It was not his own natural gifts that led people to believe in Christ, but the gift of God and his Holy Spirit.

We are encouraged by this, because God is pleased to use us, weak though we are. He understands our human limitations (and our temptation to boast about our successes!). He intends that we should depend on him in faith and trust, and to give all glory to him.

## BARABBAS—OR JESUS?

*[Pilate said] 'It is your custom for me to release to you one prisoner at the time of the Passover. Do you want me to release "the king of the Jews"?' They shouted back, 'No, not him. Give us Barabbas.'*
JOHN 18:39–40

Those who shouted loudest were probably stirred up by all who hated Roman rule. Revolts were common amongst Jewish zealots, and Barabbas was one of these. Maybe he was a terrorist, a natural murderer; maybe he had acted in what he felt was a just cause. This sort of situation is all too familiar to us in the world today.

Luke (see chapter 23:19) sees him as a murderer. Mark (see chapter 15:8) refers to him as one of the insurrectionists who had committed murder in the uprising. But John (in chapter 18:40) simply states that he had taken part in a rebellion.

It is interesting that the Aramaic name 'Barabbas' means 'son of Abba'—'son of the father'. Is it pure coincidence that, in place of him, Jesus, the 'Son of the Father' died? We cannot know. But the question of how Barabbas might have reacted is an intriguing one. What did he feel? Elation, surely. But would he not have been curious to find out what happened to Jesus? He had probably

heard of him and known of his healings and other miracles—
known him to be a good man. Did Barabbas follow the crowd to
the place of crucifixion?

If all this was so, it is not hard to imagine him saying in wonder,
'This good man dying in the place I should have occupied—Why?'
And in those words he would be speaking for sinful people like you
and me, and the many other people in all the years since then. How
I would like to think that the whole life and outlook of Barabbas
changed as he witnessed the nailing of Jesus to the cross that
would probably have been his!

That leaves us with a big question of our own: How do I feel that
the sinless Son of God died as a Sacrifice for sinners like me on that
cross?

## MOUNTAINTOP TO DESERT

*A voice came from heaven: 'You are my Son, whom I love; with
you I am well pleased.' At once the Spirit sent him out into the
desert ...*

MARK 1:11–12

What a contrast! Jesus is lovingly affirmed by his Heavenly
Father—what we might call a 'mountaintop' experience—
and then immediately given a time of severe testing. He lived
amongst the many wild animals that inhabited the land in those
days; he suffered hunger and temptation; he was cut off from
human contact—for nearly six weeks. Do we find this hard to
understand?

Evidently it was necessary for Jesus to have such a time of testing
in preparation for the great work ahead of him. Was he borne up

by his Father's words so fresh in his memory? Certainly his mind was attuned to God's Word, the Scriptures, for he used it three times to overcome Satan. And God's eyes were certainly upon his Son—for 'angels attended him' (verse 13).

Sometimes, after we have felt particularly uplifted and blessed by God, we, too, are suddenly plunged into conflict. We may be severely tempted by things we thought we had overcome; we may be dismayed and depressed. What has gone wrong? If a time of testing was necessary for Jesus, how much more so for us! It is in these 'desert' experiences that we become aware of our weakness and dependence upon God. Then, when we go forward to do some work for him, we shall be kept from pride, and he will receive the praise.

We, like Jesus, have God's Word to parry all Satan's attacks. And, just as angels ministered to Jesus, so God sends his Spirit to minister to us in our times of vulnerability. When we are brought low, let us remember our 'mountaintop' experiences and be uplifted and encouraged.

The Lord is close to the broken-hearted and saves those who are crushed in spirit (Psalm 34:18).


## ADULT EDUCATION FROM THE PROVERBS

*... for giving prudence to the simple, knowledge and discretion to the young—let the wise listen and add to their learning, and let the discerning get guidance—for understanding proverbs and parables, the sayings and riddles of the wise. The fear of the* LORD *is the beginning of knowledge, but fools despise wisdom and discipline.*

PROVERBS 1:4–7

We note here that nobody is beyond the need to learn—the simple, the young, the wise, the discerning. Learning is a lifelong process, for we can never know all in this life.

This is strikingly true when we come to acknowledge Jesus Christ as Saviour and Lord. We are as children at the beginning. At the point where we seek to reverence God and be guided by him, we have only just begun to acquire real knowledge.

The apostle Paul (in Colossians 2:2–3) speaks of the full riches of understanding which we need in order to know the mystery of God, namely Christ, in whom are hidden all the treasures of wisdom and knowledge.

It is only as we come to know Christ and learn reverent fear of God that we shall grow in understanding and spiritual maturity.

## THE BARRIER OF RICHES—MARK 10:17–22

*A man ran up to [Jesus] … 'What must I do to inherit eternal life?'*
MARK 10:17

This little episode in these verses is sad. The man was so eager, falling on his knees before Jesus. He was so sure of his goodness in keeping the commandments, yet he realised that more was needed. We read that Jesus looked at him and loved him.

Jesus, however, discerned the man's heart. There was a stumbling block there—his love of wealth. When told that he must give all that up to follow Jesus, he could not do it, and his face fell. He sadly turned away.

In loving the world more than he loved God, the man had clearly not recognised that he was breaking the first and last commandments. And he missed eternal blessing.

We are not all called to give up everything we possess to follow Christ. But if we care about these things more than about God, then we, too, shall regret it for ever.

## THE LONELINESS OF JESUS

*My soul is overwhelmed with sorrow to the point of death. Stay here and watch with me.*

MATTHEW 26:38

*He was despised and rejected by men ...*

ISAIAH 53:3

Reflecting on Jesus' agony of mind and heart and body, I think he must have felt so lonely—Jesus, of all people, without human comfort and support, scorned and derided by those he came to save. Even his closest friends slept when he needed them to watch and pray.

And to think that so soon he was to be cut off from his Father, stricken, smitten and afflicted as he took up our infirmities and carried our sorrows (Isaiah 53:4).

## PEACE—OR A SWORD?

*Do not suppose that I have come to bring peace to the earth. I did not come to bring peace, but a sword.*

MATTHEW 10:34

*The word of God is living and active. Sharper than any double-edged sword, it penetrates even to dividing soul and spirit ... it judges the thoughts and attitudes of the heart.*

HEBREWS 4:12

D o these words strike a disheartening note, threatening our cherished ideas? We are so used to finding comfort in all the sayings of Jesus about the peace he gives, especially the treasured words in John 14:27: Peace I leave with you, my peace I give you. Paul, too, speaks often of the peace of Christ. So what does Jesus mean when he says, not peace, but a sword? Do we have a contradiction here?

I think not. Jesus does not contradict himself; but he does make a distinction. He does not promise peace in the *world*—and we have plenty of evidence that this is an impossibility—but peace in our *hearts*. This is clear from Jesus' words in John 16:33: 'I have told you these things that in me you may have peace. In this world you will have trouble. But take heart! I have overcome the world.'

Christ brought a sword against materialism and sin. It is not to be peace at any price. If we put worldly considerations before the service of God, we sin against him. Christ wields the sword of the Spirit— which is the Word of God—against anything that keeps us from him.

Human nature needs this sword. The thoughts and attitudes of the heart, biased towards sin, need a radical change. This change has already been made possible by Christ's bearing of sin on the cross. Peace comes only through believing in him, and all that this entails.

## BLIND OBEDIENCE

*The LORD answered Moses, 'Is the LORD's arm too short? You will now see whether or not what I say will come true for you.'*
NUMBERS 11:23

M oses is questioning what the Lord has told him to do. It seems impossible. Here we see in Moses, not that he had unwavering faith in God at all times, but that he obeyed God in spite of any doubts he had. The next verse begins, 'So Moses went out …' He was prepared to go out in obedient faith. However difficult it was to understand God's purposes, he believed that it was indeed God himself speaking.

There is a lesson for us here: Our faith may waver, and we sometimes find it difficult to believe in God's power and his promises. But when God commands, we are expected to obey, to act on his word. That is real trust, and God will honour our faithfulness, as he did with that of Moses.

## A LUKEWARM CHURCH—REVELATION 3:15–18

*I know your deeds, that you are neither cold nor hot … so, because you are lukewarm … I am about to spit you out of my mouth. You say, 'I am rich; I have acquired wealth and do not need a thing.' But you do not realise that you are wretched, pitiful, poor, blind and naked.*

REVELATION 3:15–17

These words are spoken by the Lord to the church in Laodicea. How they must have trembled at being brought so low! After all, if we are neither cold nor hot, we are nothing. The only comfort to be found for that church is in verse 19, where God says that it is those whom he loves that he rebukes and disciplines, and he goes on to show that there is yet hope for them.

Only from God can we obtain true riches, heavenly treasure. We may delight in worldly wealth, but without God we are wretchedly poor. True wealth is in spiritual blessings. To obtain these, we need to be 'clothed with the Lord Jesus' (Romans 13:14) and keep our eyes focused on him.

Do we feel lukewarm—at least some of the time? I certainly do. If we do, we need to pray earnestly for power to witness to Christ by word and actions in our needy world. Look how often Jesus drew aside from his work for close communion with his Heavenly Father, seeking strength and wisdom for the tasks ahead. Can we, so weak and helpless, manage with less?

## A DREADFUL MISTAKE?

*The Son of Man did not come to be served, but to serve, and to give his life a ransom for many.*
MARK 10:45

There are those who insist that Jesus was at the mercy of his enemies, a helpless victim, and that his death was a terrible tragedy. They see it as complete failure in his mission to the world.

This verse contradicts thoughts like these, and it is the heart of the gospel. He was 'sent', as he himself stated on several occasions; but the essential point is that he 'came'. He existed before the world was made, and he came voluntarily and in accordance with the will of the Father.

Yes, Jesus was in an agony just before the crucifixion. But we read in Hebrews 12:2: 'who for the joy set before him endured the cross, scorning its shame'. His life was not taken from him, as some believe; he gave it out of love for sinful human beings. In John's Gospel we read of Jesus saying, 'No one takes [my life] from me, but I lay it down of my own accord. I have authority to lay it down and authority to take it up again. This command I received from my Father' (John 10:18).

This willing sacrifice is essential in demonstrating God's grace and mercy and love in achieving the salvation of his people.

## THE DARING OF BARTIMAEUS—MARK 10:46–52

*Then they came to Jericho. As Jesus and his disciples, together with a large crowd, were leaving the city, a blind man, Bartimaeus (that is, the Son of Timaeus), was sitting by the roadside begging. When he heard that it was Jesus of Nazareth, he began to shout, 'Jesus, Son of David, have mercy on me!'*

MARK 10:46–47

If you had a desperate need, like Bartimaeus in his blindness, would you have the courage and tenacity, in spite of public opposition, to call out to Jesus as he passed by?

The blind man obviously knew of Jesus, for he called him by a Messianic title, 'Son of David'; and he had some faith, for he knew that Jesus had the power and authority to heal him. So he persisted in his cry for help. The little detail of throwing aside his cloak is interesting, I think. Was it almost symbolic of his former way of life? The account tells us that he went to Jesus just as he was.

In our country we are not likely to be shouting for help in the street—except, perhaps, in dire emergency. But does this episode tell us something about prayer, and about evangelism? I think so. Bartimaeus' cry to Jesus was an opportunity for the disciples with Jesus to deepen the faith shown by the man. What did they do? They rebuked him—at least before Jesus called to him.

To Jesus, no one is insignificant, and evidence of belief in him must have warmed his heart. He called the blind man, restored his sight and told him to go on his way. But Bartimaeus chose to go Jesus' way! Might he have become a lifelong follower of our Lord? Like this blind man, can we acknowledge our need and come to Jesus, just as we are, to have our spiritual eyes opened? After a personal encounter with him, we are likely spontaneously to follow him.

## TRUE BLESSING

*Blessed are you when men hate you ... because of the Son of Man. Rejoice in that day ... because great is your reward in heaven.*
LUKE 6:22–23

Jesus does not say, 'Try to put up with persecution and hostility as best you can.' He knows that we can bear it only in his strength. So he says, 'Rejoice! Leap for joy!' Why? We shall be privileged to share in his suffering—just a fraction of what he endured for us.

When someone gives something to us, we delight to give in return. We can never repay the debt we owe Christ for his saving work for us. But we can, in some small measure, suffer willingly for the continuation of his work and for the glory of his name.

## A SAFE DISTANCE

*Peter followed [Jesus] at a distance.*
MARK 14:54

These words apply to Peter during the appearance before the high priest of Jesus at his trial.

We probably know, or hear of, people who follow Jesus at a safe distance. Maybe we ourselves do the same. Just as an earthworm leaves the tip of its tail in the soil while it ascertains whether there is a predator nearby, making sure that it can quickly withdraw at any sign of danger, so we may keep one foot in the world ready to withdraw when things get difficult or too demanding in the Christian life.

Jesus doesn't ask for half-hearted, safe, distant followers. Those who become his disciples may have to forsake all. We are to expect suffering and hardship for his sake. To follow him is to take up our cross, and that is a costly thing to do. But those who do so, and walk close to him, know a peace and fellowship that 'the world' can never offer.

## HOW CAN I BELIEVE THAT?

*The angel said ... 'Do not be afraid, Zechariah; your prayer has been heard. Your wife Elizabeth will bear you a son.' ... Zechariah asked the angel, 'How can I be sure of this? I am an old man and my wife is well on in years.' The angel answered, 'I am Gabriel. I stand in the presence of God, and I have been sent to speak to you and tell you the good news. And now you will be silent and not able to speak until the day this happens, because you did not believe my words ...'*
LUKE 1:13, 18–20

I think many readers can identify with Zechariah's doubt. After all, the angel was declaring that God would do something humanly impossible! Yet the angel spoke with authority, so Zechariah was punished for his unbelief. Why should anybody expect the God of all creation to confine himself to human limitations?

It seems to be a common failing that we do not really expect God to do that which is beyond our understanding. We find evidence of this in both the Old Testament and the New, and we find it amongst Christians today. When something amazing happens after prayer, we are surprised, instinctively first putting it down to coincidence. We acknowledge the wonder of God's grace and power; we know from the Bible that he hears prayer offered in faith; yet we do not really expect him to act. It is a difficult matter, because sometimes—often, in fact—there is no apparent answer, or a different response to that for which we hoped. But can we not trust God? Having done our best to be attuned to God's will, and having prayed in faith, we can go on our way in greater lightness of heart, leaving the matter with him. It is true that we are taught to persevere in prayer, but we can let go of the worry each time we have brought our trouble to God.


## THE PSALMIST'S HONESTY—PSALM 35

*May all who gloat over my distress be put to shame and confusion.*

PSALM 35:26

This psalm is so honest. It is full of pleas to God to punish those who are making the writer's life intolerable. We tend not to sing or recite such psalms in church, perhaps because we don't like admitting that we ourselves do sometimes feel like this. This is a real-life experience.

The important thing is that these feelings are addressed to God, with praise and trust for his help in our need. Surely it is to God that we can allow ourselves to pour out our bewilderment, anguish and bitterness. We do sometimes want God to punish those who hurt us, our loved ones or others in the world (especially if they do not apologise!). But we need to recognise and acknowledge our own guilt, too.

We cannot pretend before God. Only as we bring our feelings to him can he heal us and change us, and enable us to forgive others as he forgives us.

## SIGNPOSTS—THOUGHTS FROM JOHN 14:1–7 AND PSALM 119:105

*Jesus answered, 'I am the way and the truth and the life. No one comes to the Father except through me.'*
JOHN 14:6
*Your word is a lamp to my feet and a light for my path.*
PSALM 119:105

Whenever I read either of these two passages, I recall a certain event in my life. I was on my way to stay with friends in a remote part of Sussex. It was early evening when I set out, and I was enjoying the scenery as I drove along the well-signposted route. But then I came to a junction with no signpost. I had no idea which way to take. The further I travelled, the more convinced I became that I was on the wrong road. Once this doubt took hold of me I lost all interest in my surroundings, beautiful though they were. It was beginning to get dark and, worst of all, I was very low on petrol.

The only house I came to was deserted; there were no other cars; and I had no mobile phone. What was I to do? Panic! Would I really be stranded for the night in the middle of the country? Wait! Hadn't I a direct line to God? I prayed. Within a few minutes I heard a car approaching. It stopped. The driver not only knew the track I was making for, but led me to it—only a few hundred yards away! I truly believe that I had been sent one of God's messengers.

Jesus, in his discourse in the upper room before his crucifixion, told his disciples that he was going away, and that they knew the way he was going. Thomas, however, did not know the way, or where Jesus was going. Perhaps he spoke for all the others, and how troubled they must have been!

We trust quite naturally in signposts along the road. Can we not trust Jesus, who is himself the way to the Father and to the kingdom of heaven? We have someone to follow on our whole journey through life, and we can travel with untroubled hearts. And, with the light of Jesus, we shall most certainly reach our destination in complete safety.

## DRAMA IN HEAVEN

*Holy, holy, holy is the Lord God Almighty, who was and is and is to come.*

REVELATION 4:8

The whole of this chapter is full of the richest imagery. It is as if John cannot find anything big enough, dramatic enough, to express the majesty of God. How could he? To describe God in all his glory is beyond the reach of any vocabulary we have.

We are made very aware of the holiness of God. Sometimes it seems that the church has lost the sense of awe, the reverent fear that comes from the knowledge of our unworthiness to approach

God, sinful as we are. Yes, God is love, and he is Father, and this is all very comfortable to live with. But are we in danger of forgetting that he is also a righteous and holy Judge?

Only by the cleansing blood of Jesus, accepted in humility and thankfulness, can we approach 'the throne of God'. May we never lose sight of the vast, illuminating concept of eternity and God's sovereignty over all.


## SUCH A SHORT SPAN ON EARTH—THOUGHTS ON PSALM 39

*I will put a muzzle on my mouth as long as the wicked are in my presence.*

*Show me, O LORD, my life's end and the number of my days; let me know how fleeting my life is.*

PSALM 39:1, 4

This psalm was written during a time of illness, thought to be a rebuke from God.

It seems that the writer no longer wants to live; nor does he dare to speak out against God lest he dishonour him before 'the wicked'. Recognising the shortness of this life, he sees the worthlessness of worldly wealth.

Whether or not we are ill or depressed, it is good to take the long view. Following the psalmist's train of thought, perhaps we, too, often feel unable to express doubts and fears in case we undermine the faith of others; yet there are many things that trouble us because we do not understand. Maybe open discussion of such problems, backed up by prayer, would help, rather than hinder, those very people.

Like the psalmist, we need to realise our mortality and get our priorities right, living to the full before God, for all too soon that life will be over. All our bustling about, and our concern for financial and material security is, to a large extent, futile. All our ills are an inevitable part of our human condition. Most of us do not see them as a rebuke from God, though he may show us that we sometimes unwittingly cause them. If our hope is in God, and if we trust him, then we may see his love in all our suffering, and learn to discern his will in it all.

The writer of this psalm asks God to look away from him. Do you want that? Sinful and weak as we are, is it not better for God to know us through and through? Surely he is willing and able to put right what is wrong and change us so that we become what he means us to be! He alone can cause us to grow in grace and holiness before we depart this life.

## THE GLORY OF CHRIST

*The Word became flesh and made his dwelling among us. We have seen his glory, the glory of the One and Only ...*
JOHN 1:14

As in Revelation 4:8, we are made aware of the holiness of God, this time as seen in Jesus Christ. John the Baptist is testifying about Jesus. The whole of this chapter is awesome. The Baptist states, 'I have seen and I testify that this is the Son of God' (verse 34)—the one who made him feel too humble even to untie his sandals. Isn't that a lovely detail?

Are we too casual, too familiar, when talking to Jesus? When people came face to face with him, many fell at his feet—and he accepted their worship. But he is friend to us, as well as Lord and Saviour. Nevertheless, we do well to remember that he has existed with God from the beginning; he is the agent of creation; he is with God and declares God. Nathanael says to him, 'You are the Son of God; you are the King of Israel' (verse 49). Even this early in Jesus' ministry, some recognised who he was, discerning in him an awesome quality of authority.

## TAKE NOTHING FOR THE JOURNEY—LUKE 9:1–6

*Jesus told the twelve, 'Take nothing for the journey—no staff, no bag, no bread, no money, no extra tunic.'*
LUKE 9:3

If, like me, you feel insecure setting out on a journey without all the things you consider essential, then you will marvel at these disciples who, in obedience and faith, went off on their mission taking nothing. And, as far as we know, they managed!

They were bound to meet with success in this venture for at least four reasons:

Jesus called them;

Jesus gave them power;

Jesus sent them with his instructions;

They went in total dependence on God for their needs.

Sometimes we fail in what we do for the Lord. Perhaps it was a self-appointed task, not founded on prayer; or we did not listen to the Lord's instructions; or God had not called us to that particular task. Maybe we set out without seeking his guidance and power, making our own decisions and arrangements. Did we rely on our own resources—material and spiritual?

How important it is to pray before action is taken and decisions made! What a difference it would make if all Christians drew near to Jesus at the start of each day, like messengers waiting for their assignments! We would do well to ask, 'What do you want of us this day?' Then we would do only what he called us to undertake, and we would know that his strength and wisdom would be available to us.

I find it important, too, to make sure, through prayer, that I am not encumbered with yesterday's problems or today's anxieties, free to set off joyfully on the road marked out for me. It is good to know we are responding to his will and relying on his strength. We have only to obey, and we can't do that unless we have first listened.

In verse 10 we read that the disciples reported back to the Lord, after which he took them aside to rest. We can follow their example: at the end of each day we review with the Lord how things have gone. Then we receive refreshment and rest in his presence. And what joy if we hear his words, 'Well done, good and faithful servant'!

## THE DISHONEST TENANTS—MARK 12:1–9

*He had one left to send, a son, whom he loved. He sent him last of all, saying, 'They will respect my son.'*
*But the tenants said to one another, 'This is the heir. Come, let's kill him, and the inheritance will be ours.' So they took him and killed him, and threw him out of the vineyard.*
MARK 12:6–8

This well-known parable seems to be the story of failure from beginning to end. Each of the servants sent to collect what was due to the owner of the vineyard was killed by the tenants. Finally the owner sent his son, but he, too, was killed. The end result was that those tenants were to be put to death.

The son in the parable represents Jesus. All God's prophets had failed. When they proclaimed God's word of warning, they were ignored, tortured and even killed.

However, the end of this story is uniquely different from that in the parable: It was God's purpose that his Son should die for his people, for only in that way could he show his love and draw them to himself. 'Greater love has no one than this, that he lay down his life for his friends,' says Jesus to his disciples (John 15:13). This was God's redeeming love—to set us free from slavery to sin, to accept us into his kingdom and bestow upon us the gift of eternal life.

The Lord 'is not wanting anyone to perish, but everyone to come to repentance' (2 Peter 3:9). His final act to save not just his chosen people, the Jews, but people from all nations, was to send Jesus to die as their substitute. How wonderful is his love and grace in salvation!

## THE POWER OF PRAYER—ACTS 12:1–17

*The night before Herod was to bring him to trial, Peter was sleeping between two soldiers, bound with two chains, and sentries stood guard at the entrance. Suddenly an angel of the Lord appeared and a light shone in the cell. He struck Peter on the side and woke him up. 'Quick, get up!' he said, and the chains fell off Peter's wrists.*

ACTS 12:6–7

This account is full of interesting detail. Do read it all. But let's concentrate here on two points to apply personally.

Verses 1–11: Peter was behind locked doors because of his faith, bound with chains, lying in darkness, asleep in the peace of God. Let us imagine ourselves in a prison of unbelief. Our chains and darkness are unforgiven sin; our sleep is passive acceptance; our locked doors are barriers against God. How are we to be woken to an awareness of our situation and set free? Only through one who is greater than the angel that woke Peter—the Son of God, Jesus Christ. He jogs us into recognising our need; brings light into our darkness, loosens the chains of sin and calls us to follow him. He gives a new sense of direction to our lives. Doors open that were locked before—doors of understanding—and we have new vision, new life.

When all this happens, we realise that the hand of God was on us, in our hearts and lives. How did this come about? Someone, somewhere, was praying for us, as the church was praying for Peter. We may never know the angel who first stirred us in our sleep; but God knows. He came to us and will be with us always.

Lord Jesus Christ, may we who know you be faithful in prayer for those who do not know you, so that they may be set free and come into God's kingdom of light and love.

Verses 12–17: The other disciples were gathered together to pray for Peter's release, but they had evidently not yet learned the power of prayer in spite of Jesus' teaching. Here they were praying, but they seemed to lack faith. Peter knocks at the door after his amazing escape, and they cannot believe their eyes when they find him standing there!

Is this a picture of your prayer life and mine? We claim to pray in faith, but sometimes fail to realise that it was God who answered our request. Why do we hold on to our own limited vision of what God can do? Perhaps we should engage more in expectant prayer and discover the wonders that God can do. It may be true of us that we 'do not have, because [we] do not ask God' (James 4:2). The more we learn to recognise God in action, the more our faith will grow.

We may be amazed at the way God works, but we need never doubt that he does so.

## THE VINE AND THE BRANCHES—JOHN 15:1–4

*I am the true vine and my Father is the gardener. He cuts off every branch in me that bears no fruit, while every branch that does bear fruit he trims clean so that it will be even more fruitful.*
JOHN 15:1–2

Pruning is never likely to be a comfortable process! When a rose bush is cut back before the winter it looks ugly and useless; it is hard to visualise it ever flowering again, or even surviving.

Suffering is painful—and often ugly. But pruning has a purpose: it is so that the rose bush (or the vine in this passage) will bear fruit. The more it is cut back, the more the fruit. Does this go some way to explaining suffering in 'good' people and innocent people—that there can be a purpose in it?

If we trust our Divine Gardener we will accept this cutting back, this apparent damage to ourselves. We recoil at the idea of being cut off altogether because we bear no fruit, and rightly so. This is completely negative. But we can, and do, rebel sometimes when suffering hits us; we do not like to be hurt, either physically or emotionally. But, as Amy Carmichael has famously said, 'In acceptance lies peace.' A certain amount of looking ahead in hope is required for that, as well as trust in our Heavenly Father—and, of course, abiding in Jesus, the vine.

Paul writes in Romans 15:13 of 'peace in believing'. Yes, if we believe in God's love for us, then we shall allow him to do his work in all our trials and suffering—and be at peace.

There is a saying by G.K. Chesterton, part of which states: 'An adventure is an inconvenience rightly considered.' I think this can apply just as much to real trials as to minor inconveniences. How good it would be if we could regard the whole of life, with all its ups and downs, as an adventure with God!

## UNLOVELY SUFFERING—ISAIAH 53

*He grew up before him like a tender shoot, and like a root out of dry ground. He had no beauty or majesty to attract us to him, nothing in his appearance that we should desire him. He was despised and rejected by men, a man of sorrows, and familiar with suffering. Like one from whom men hide their faces he was despised, and we esteemed him not.*

ISAIAH 53:2–3

Does this remind you of anyone? Yes, this wonderful passage concerns the Messiah who was to come. 'Our message' (verse 1) is the good news about salvation through Jesus Christ. Our Lord's coming sufferings are so tenderly described here, so exactly foretold, that we can be moved to tears.

It is a sad fact that we are often embarrassed by a person's grief or disability, and especially by mental illness. It's easier to look the other way than to try to respond, to confront it. Perhaps that is why there is a tendency amongst some people to make fun of disabled individuals; it replaces fear.

I think of a young man that I see often on the beach. He is

uncoordinated and makes strange faces and gestures. Yet he is clean and tidy, and good-looking, too. My heart yearns to make contact with him in his strange isolation, yet I fear to approach him, not knowing how he would behave towards me, or even if he could speak intelligibly. Nor do I know if he wants to associate with anyone.

People could not take Jesus' tremendous offering of himself in suffering, and they hid their faces. Would we have done the same? But he died for sinful people like you and me! Such love is hard to accept. Of all human suffering and degradation, crucifixion must surely be the worst. Jesus did not look the heroic, authoritative figure people wanted and expected him to be. Yet, because he bore the sin of many, he will be satisfied in the final outcome of having achieved their redemption.

## LIGHT-BEARERS
*You are the light of the world ... Let your light shine.*
MATTHEW 5:14–16

I am like the moon—It has no light, only the reflection of the sun's light! Yes, but I can shine in the world with the light that I receive from Christ.

I am thinking today of a diamond. Basically, it is a hard lump of rock—and a jagged one at that! Its beauty is only in the brilliance of reflected light from many facets that are the result of much careful cutting away of surplus material. The more facets there are, the greater the sparkle and value of the gem.

If we are to be light in the world, we need this cutting away by the Divine Craftsman—freeing from sin, attachment to worldly possessions, pride, superficiality, and so on. This may be a painful process.

Another picture that springs to mind is of a glass paperweight which was given to me—such a disappointment when I first opened the box! It is absolutely colourless. But on the base, a craftsman has cut the shape of flowers. Wherever I put it, the cut parts make it reflect many colours from the objects around it. It is constantly changing, and a real delight to look at.

You and I may be plain glass, but once our Creator gets to work on us we can reflect his beauty and light, pleasing to him and a blessing to others.

## A GOOD FRIDAY MEDITATION—THE AGONIES OF JESUS

*Let us fix our eyes on Jesus, the author and perfecter of our faith, who for the joy set before him endured the cross, scorning its shame, and sat down at the right hand of the throne of God. Consider him who endured such opposition from sinful men, so that you will not grow weary and lose heart.*

HEBREWS 12:2–3

*D istrust*—Throughout his ministry, there were those who refused to believe in him or his teaching. We know something of what it is like to experience disbelief and hostility in our witness, and to be accused of wrong motives.

Do we suffer this willingly for anyone? Our Lord did.

*Unpopularity*—Many turned away from him because he was uncompromising concerning the uncomfortable truth. We may have been tempted to water down the gospel message to avoid alienation by those who would find it unpalatable.

Can we stand boldly for the whole truth? Our Lord did.

*Desertion*—His friends fell asleep, and later ran away, in his hour of need. Yet Jesus' love for them did not waver. We count on our friends when we are in trouble, and some go out of their minds when denied love. Jesus must have felt very alone in all the weary hours of his trial, but he was resolute in doing his Father's will.

Would we willingly suffer desertion for the sake of the truth? Our Lord did.

*Fear*—The dread of the suffering on the cross was physical, mental and spiritual—yet we are told that he had joy for the final outcome! He was laying down his life of his own accord. But the sharing of our humanity meant inevitable suffering—cruel pain, bruises and wounds, mockery, the painful crown of thorns, the lashings, the nails driven in, the indignity, the thirst and the slow dying. We know how we would fear any one of these. We know how we feel when faced with any really difficult situation, none in any way comparable with Jesus' work of salvation.

Do we take on really costly work for God? Our Lord did.

*Abandonment*—Jesus was bearing our sin, and God cannot look upon sin. He had always been so close to the Father, and now he felt forsaken. Darkness came over the whole land, blotting out even the Light of the World. Jesus cried, 'Why?' Even he experienced doubt: He was tempted in every respect as we are so that he might sympathise with our weakness (see Hebrews 4:15).

Would we risk abandonment for the sake of our principles? Our Lord did.

*Betrayal*—Judas valued thirty pieces of silver more than his relationship with Jesus. He was instrumental in causing the death of the one who offered him LIFE.

Would we choose as a friend one likely to betray us? Our Lord did.

*Violence*—Jesus was now in the hands of his executioners and tormentors, and they did not spare him. Yet he prayed that God would forgive them. Jesus, who preached peace, rebuked the disciple who struck with his sword one of the soldiers that came to arrest him, Jesus. He was a healer to the last, healing the wounded man.

Would we, at such a time, feel love that could heal? Our Lord did.

*Scorn*—Jesus was dying for the very people who poured scorn on him. They were oblivious to the fact that this man was giving his life to save theirs.

Could we give costly love to those who scorned us? Our Lord did.

*Callous indifference*—The soldiers at the foot of the cross gambled for the victim's possessions, blind to the suffering one. But Jesus showed no malice.

Could we forebear to cry out at such indifference? Our Lord did.

*A sorrowing mother*—Jesus must always have known that his work would cause her suffering. Her pain and sorrow now would have been torment to him. Even in the midst of his own agony, he was concerned for her welfare.

Are we willing to put God's will first? Our Lord was.